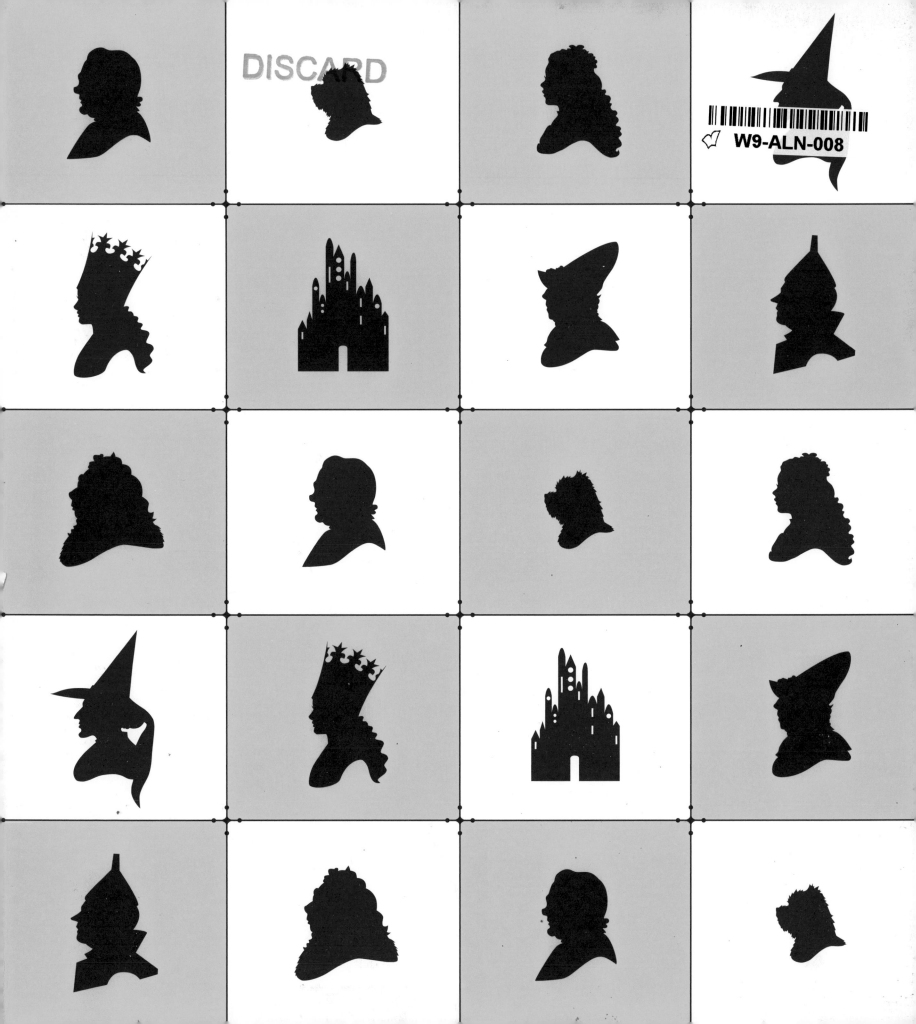

DISCARD

W9-ALN-008

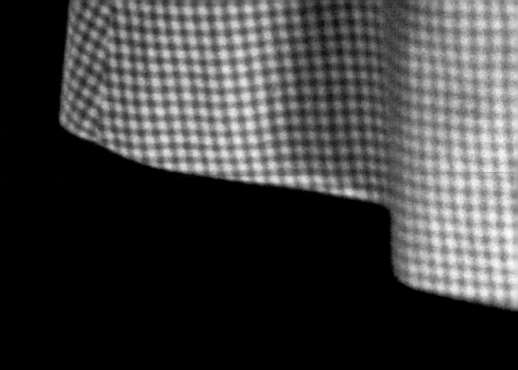

LIFE BOOKS

Managing Editor
Robert Sullivan

Director of Photography
Barbara Baker Burrows

Creative Director
Anke Stohlmann/Li'l Robin
Design, Inc.

Deputy Picture Editor
Christina Lieberman

Copy Chief
Barbara Gogan

Copy Editors
Don Armstrong, Parlan McGaw

Writer-Reporters
Michelle DuPré, Marilyn Fu,
Amy Lennard Goehner

Photo Associate
Sarah Cates

Editorial Associate
Courtney Mifsud

Consulting Picture Editors
Mimi Murphy (Rome),
Tala Skari (Paris)

TIME INC. PREMEDIA

Richard K. Prue (Director),
Brian Fellows (Manager),
Richard Shaffer (Production),
Keith Aurelio, Jen Brown,
Charlotte Coco, Liz Grover,
Kevin Hart, Mert Kerimoglu,
Rosalie Khan, Patricia Koh,
Marco Lau, Brian Mai, Po Fung
Ng, Rudi Papiri, Robert Pizaro,
Barry Pribula, Clara Renauro,
Vaune Trachtman

TIME HOME ENTERTAINMENT

President Jim Childs

**Vice President, Brand & Digital
Strategy** Steven Sandonato

Executive Director, Marketing Services
Carol Pittard

**Executive Director, Retail & Special
Sales** Tom Mifsud

Executive Publishing Director
Joy Bomba

**Director, Bookazine Development
& Marketing** Laura Adam

Vice President, Finance
Vandana Patel

Publishing Director
Megan Pearlman

Associate General Counsel Helen Wan

Assistant Director, Special Sales
Ilene Schreider

Senior Book Production Manager
Susan Chodakiewicz

Brand Manager Roshni Patel

Associate Prepress Manager
Alex Voznesenskiy

Associate Project Manager
Stephanie Braga

Editorial Director
Stephen Koepp

Senior Editor
Roe D'Angelo

Copy Chief
Rina Bander

Design Manager
Anne-Michelle Gallero

Editorial Operations
Gina Scauzillo

Special thanks: Katherine Barnet,
Brad Beatson, Jeremy Biloon,
Dana Campolattaro, Rose
Cirrincione, Natalie Ebel, Assu
Etsubneh, Mariana Evans, Christine
Font, Susan Hettleman, Hillary
Hirsch, David Kahn, Amy Mangus,
Kimberly Marshall, Nina Mistry,
Dave Rozzelle, Ricardo Santiago,
Adriana Tierno

Copyright © 2014 Time Home
Entertainment Inc.

Published by LIFE Books,
an imprint of Time Home
Entertainment Inc.
135 West 50th Street,
New York, New York 10020

All rights reserved. No part of
this book may be reproduced in
any form or by any electronic
or mechanical means, including
information storage and retrieval
systems, without permission in
writing from the publisher, except
by a reviewer, who may quote
brief passages in a review.

ISBN 10: 1-61893-103-2
ISBN 13: 978-1-61893-103-0
Library of Congress Control
Number: 2013956970

"LIFE" is a registered trademark
of Time Inc.

We welcome your comments
and suggestions about LIFE Books.
Please write to us at:
LIFE Books
Attention: Book Editors
PO Box 11016
Des Moines, IA 50336-1016

If you would like to order any of our
hardcover Collector's Edition books,
please call us at 1-800-327-6388
(Monday through Friday, 7 a.m.–
8 p.m., or Saturday, 7 a.m.–6 p.m.,
Central Time).

Page 1: Emerging from the pages.
PHOTOGRAPH FROM MGM/KOBAL/
ART RESOURCE, NY

Pages 2–3: Munchkinland
in Culver City, California.
PHOTOGRAPH FROM MGM/PHOTOFEST

These pages: The world's most
famous footwear, on the feet of
Judy Garland.
PHOTOGRAPH FROM MGM/PHOTOFEST

Silhouette illustrations of
Wizard of Oz **icons:** ISABEL TALSMA

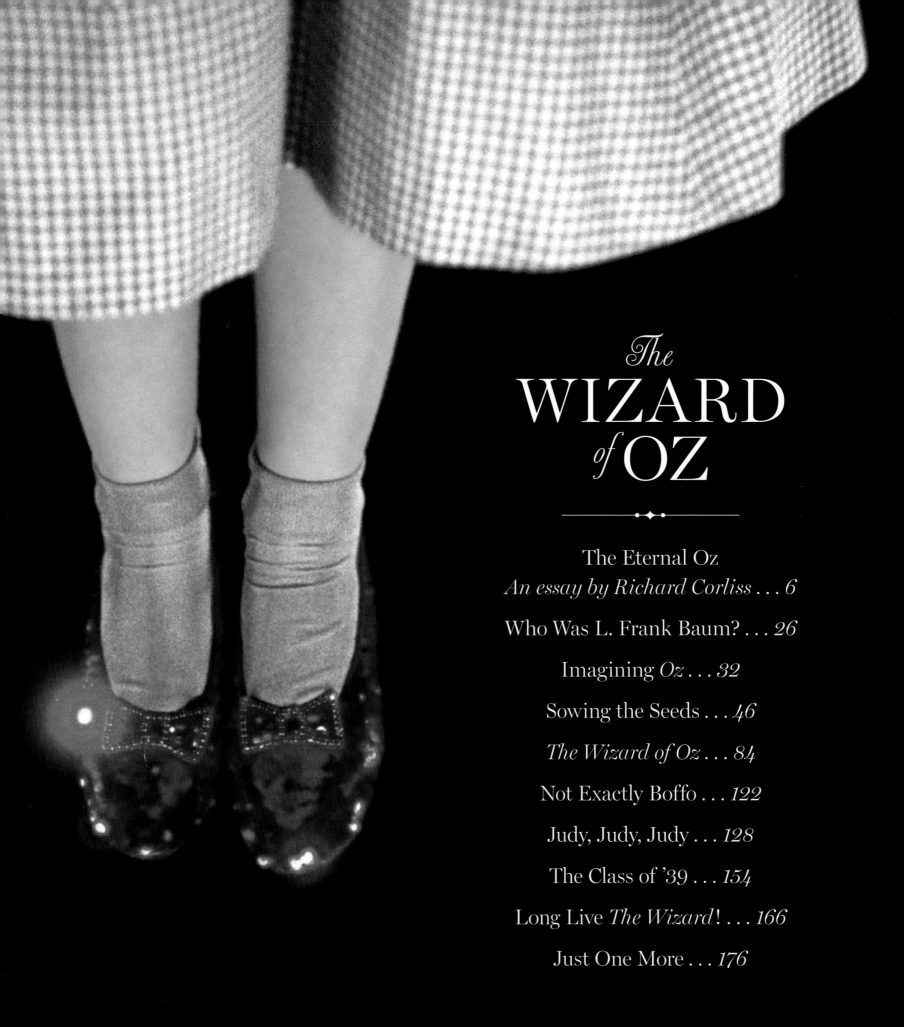

The
WIZARD
of OZ

◆

EVERETT

The ETERNAL OZ

First on the pages of one special book and then on the screen in a very special movie, this story gained—*earned*—immortality. Our film-history wizard, longtime *Time* magazine critic **RICHARD CORLISS,** explains it all. *Of course L. Frank Baum wrote the book, then the first great promoter to take* The Wizard of Oz *to another level was Broadway producer Fred R. Hamlin, who enjoyed a great stage success (opposite) in 1902.*

L. Frank Baum's book, published in 1900, was a smash, generating scores of sequels—a baker's dozen written by the man himself and then more by others. That was merely the start. In 1902 the author wrote the lyrics and libretto for a lavish stage musical that, after further development, ran on Broadway for 464 performances. Baum also turned the books into a traveling show that he narrated, as the Wizard, with the help of actors, film strips and magic-lantern slides—these were the money-losing *Fairylogue and Radio-Plays.* In 1910 the first movie version appeared, featuring a young Bebe Daniels in the role of Dorothy. In 1925 another silent-film adaptation hit the screen, costarring Oliver Hardy as the Tin Woodman.

Since then, international film remakes have run the gamut from *O* to *Z* worldwide. *The Wiz,* a black-cast Broadway musical, was filmed in 1978 with Diana Ross as Dorothy and Michael Jackson as the Scarecrow. The Disney studio mounted a sequel (the 1985 *Return to Oz*) and a prequel (2013's *Oz the Great and Powerful*).

Back on Broadway, the musical *Wicked,* a revisionist tribute to the Wicked Witch of the West, based upon Gregory Maguire's fascinating novel, has been enthralling audiences for a decade.

Yet when most people hear the phrase *The Wizard of Oz,* their minds and hearts leap directly to the 1939 MGM film starring a 16-year-old Judy Garland. Millions of movie lovers warm retrospectively to the Technicolor splendor of the Emerald City, to witches good and wicked, to the fearsome Wizard, to Munchkins and monkeys and poppies—and Toto too—with the whole indelible dreamscape spun from a lonely girl's fraught wish to be somewhere over the rainbow.

Multiple generations, of every age, truly from toddler to centenarian, know the film's dialogue by heart. "Toto, I've a feeling we're not in Kansas anymore"; "I'll get you, my pretty, and your little dog, too!"; and "There's no place like home"—all are included on the American Film Institute's list of Top 100 movie quotes. Harold Arlen and E.Y. (Yip) Harburg's songs have nestled permanently in every fan's internal jukebox, suitable for retrieval in the most peculiar circumstances. We all sing "Over the Rainbow" to ourselves, but also: In England, when former prime minister Margaret Thatcher died in April 2013, her political detractors waged a campaign to propel the Munchkins' song "Ding-Dong! The Witch Is Dead" to No. 2 on the British music charts. It hit No. 1 in the U.K. iTunes store.

Was it a great movie? Of course it was. And yet, nominated for six Academy Awards, *The Wizard of Oz* won only two, for Original Score and Original Song (yes, "Over the Rainbow"). Mind you, 1939 is commonly acknowledged as a vintage year for Hollywood films, maybe the best ever—as a later chapter of our book will emphasize. Of the 10 finalists for Best Picture, *Gone with the Wind* won eight awards, including the big one, defeating three other powerful adaptations of famous novels: *Wuthering Heights, Of Mice and Men* and *Goodbye, Mr. Chips.* Frank Capra's political rouser *Mr. Smith Goes to Washington* secured a nomination, as did two transcendent weepies, *Dark Victory* with Bette Davis and *Love Affair* with Irene Dunne. Foraging beyond the usual stately dramas, the Academy also cited a western, John Ford's *Stagecoach* (which made John Wayne a star), and Ernst Lubitsch's romantic comedy *Ninotchka* ("Garbo laughs!"); both films are close to being the definitive examples of their genres. Oh, and a musical: *The Wizard of Oz.*

With the years, the movie has, if anything, grown larger. What film needs Oscars when its awards shelf keeps filling decades after its original release? The trophies are of all sorts; to prove the point, let's consider three. A *People* magazine poll of the century's favorite movies rated *The Wizard of Oz* as No. 1., tied with *The Godfather.* Okay; fine; makes sense. When the British magazine *Total Film* picked The 23 Weirdest Films of All Time, *The Wizard* was again, and startlingly, the winner, beating out such authentic indie oddities as *Eraserhead, Being John Malkovich, Donnie Darko* and *Pi.* Okay. That's cool. And in 2001, experts from the Recording Industry Association of America chose "Over the Rainbow" as the top song of the 20th century. This too makes sense.

All of it makes sense, but only when considering the wonderful *Wizard of Oz.*

THE MUSEUM OF THE CITY OF NEW YORK/ART RESOURCE, NY

Anna Fitzhugh (a stage name of Anna Powell) *was in the chorus of the Hamlin musical, playing alternately a Munchkin, a Snow Boy or whatever was needed. She threw a dinner for the cast at the Ansonia Hotel in New York City in 1903, and blessedly there was a camera in the room.*

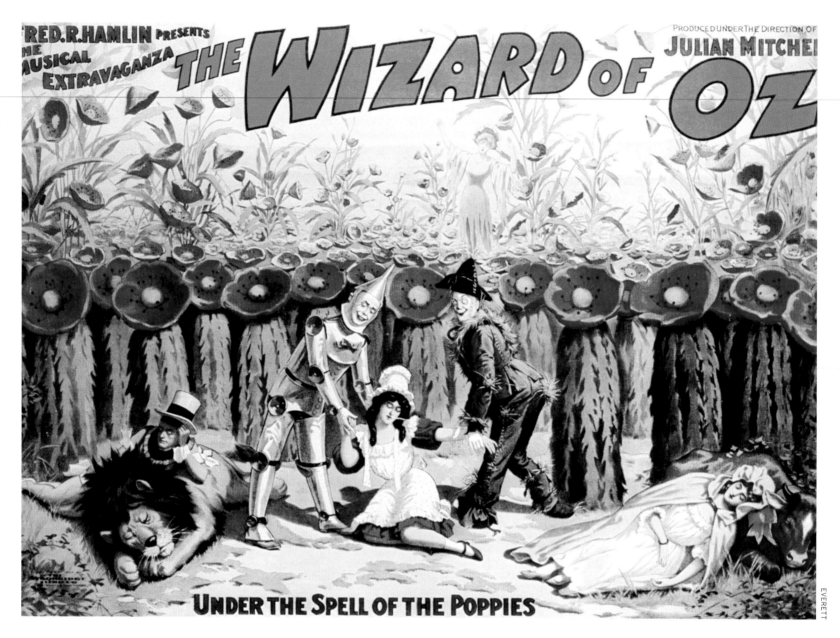

FRED.R.HAMLIN PRESENTS THE MUSICAL EXTRAVAGANZA THE **WIZARD OF OZ**

PRODUCED UNDER THE DIRECTION OF JULIAN MITCHELL

UNDER THE SPELL OF THE POPPIES

EVERETT

The success of *The Wizard of Oz* was neither sure nor immediate. Hollywood's most ambitious previous attempt at a live-action fairy tale—Paramount's 1933 *Alice in Wonderland,* with Gary Cooper as the White Knight, Cary Grant as the Mock Turtle and W.C. Fields (who was the top choice for MGM's Wizard) as Humpty-Dumpty—had foundered at the box office. What spurred MGM to make a musical version of the Baum book was the popular and critical favor for *Snow White and the Seven Dwarfs,* Walt Disney's first animated feature, which was a big hit in 1937. In a promotional book for exhibitors, MGM trumpeted the achievement of another studio: "You are Presenting the

Many of the things that were highlighted in the MGM 1939 musical were highlighted much earlier in that first stage musical, and MGM without question examined and dissected the Hamlin production—even unto the poppies. They also considered rehiring some of the actors, but finally decided to skew younger.

Greatest Marvels, Splendors and Wonders on the Screen since the Extraordinary *Snow White*," adding for clarity that "*The Wizard of Oz* is Played by a Cast of LIVING ACTORS! It is not a Cartoon Picture."

MGM would boast that it had spent "$3 million" (a production budget gives the figure as being $2,769,230.30) on a film in a genre, the musical fantasy, which had never produced a live-action hit. Plus: This was a movie with no stars. The opening credits expend only one card on the names of the eight principal players—Garland, Frank Morgan as the Wizard (and Professor Marvel), Ray Bolger as the Scarecrow (and Hunk the farmhand), Bert Lahr as the Cowardly Lion (and Zeke), Jack Haley as the Tin Man (and Hickory), Billie Burke as Glinda the Good Witch, Margaret Hamilton as the Wicked Witch (and Almira Gulch) and Charley Grapewin as Uncle Henry. (Clara Blandick, in the crucial role of Auntie Em, was not listed, though "the Munchkins," a.k.a. the Singer Midgets, were.) Morgan had been a reliable MGM comic foil; Bolger, Lahr, Haley and Burke were seasoned stage performers. Garland would soon achieve her own legend, intimately tied to this film, but wasn't a household name yet—she sure wasn't Shirley Temple. And Hamilton, who won a curious renown for her role—decades later, she'd sign her autograph "WWW" for Wicked Witch of the West—was a nobody.

And behind the cameras, even more chaos and more anonymity: *The Wizard of Oz* stands today as a conundrum of a different color, a masterpiece made by anonymous craftsmen. A dozen screenwriters worked on the script, with the credit finally going to Noel Langley, Florence Ryerson and Edgar Allan Woolf, all of whom had worked on earlier Judy Garland films but each of whom is notable for little else. Renown for the geniuses who brought *Oz* to riotous life, including art director William A. Horning, makeup artist Jack Dawn and special-effects maven A. Arnold (Buddy) Gillespie, really doesn't extend far beyond this film. Mervyn LeRoy, who had established his name as the director of such crime films as *Little Caesar* and *I Am a Fugitive from a Chain Gang*, was the producer of record; but the film's guiding hand belonged to associate producer Arthur Freed, who received no screen credit. It was

Freed (later the producer of MGM's finest musicals) who shepherded *The Wizard* from first concept to finished film. And nobody knows it or credits it.

Victor Fleming ought to be famous, if only for his work on 1939 films; he directed *Gone with the Wind* and *The Wizard of Oz*. Yet he is absent from most critics' Hollywood Pantheon, though Michael Sragow makes a strong case in his biography *Victor Fleming: An American Movie Master*. Assigned to his first musical and first color film because of his smart handling of two children's adventure movies, *Treasure Island* and *Captains Courageous,* Fleming steered the *Oz* shooting until David O. Selznick called on him to replace George Cukor as director of *GWTW*.

All of these directors—Fleming, Cukor, Sam Wood—were on both of those busy sets in 1938, and Fleming is inally listed as the director of both of these classics, perhaps because he was tough enough. A man's man whom Sragow calls "the real Rhett Butler," Fleming could flare into bullying, even sadistic behavior. He once slapped Garland for giggling during a scene. In a near-tragedy, Margaret Hamilton caught fire during the Munchkinland sequence; after six weeks' absence from the film, she wore a glove on her right hand to cover the exposed nerves. When she returned to the set, Fleming grabbed the hand hard. "Well, the pain was so unbearable," Hamilton recalled, "that I almost passed out. 'It looks fine,' he said." Fleming's tough-guy persona pushed both *The Wizard of Oz* and *Gone with the Wind* forward, and they both look fine. Judge him as you will.

After an unusually long shooting schedule of 108 days, and furious fiddling in postproduction, *The Wizard of Oz* premiered on August 12, 1939, in an unlikely place: Oconomowoc, Wisconsin, a small city about 30 miles from Milwaukee. The film opened at Grauman's Chinese Theatre in Hollywood on August 15, and two days later at Broadway's Capitol Theatre in New York City, where Garland and her frequent costar Mickey Rooney performed after the screening, as they would for the next several weeks. The reviews were mostly positive, with *Time*'s critic opining, "As long as *The Wizard of Oz* sticks to whimsy and magic, it floats in the same rare atmosphere of enchantment that distinguished Walt Disney's *Snow White and the Seven Dwarfs . . .* Lavish in sets, adult in humor, it is a Broadway spectacle translated into make-believe."

But the acclaim didn't instantly translate into big bucks for MGM. In its initial release, the movie earned about $3 million—the 10th-highest-grossing picture of 1939, behind *Gone with the Wind,* of course, but also *Mr. Smith Goes to Washington* and *Goodbye, Mr. Chips,* as well as the Garland-Rooney *Babes in Arms*—to finish in the red after studio overhead and exhibitors' fees were factored in. Not until its 1949 rerelease did the movie enter the profit side of MGM's ledgers.

Ah, but then *The Wizard of Oz* notched another— probably its greatest—distinction: It achieved classic status through annual TV showings. Viewers whom the film had beguiled as children watched it with their kids, and on and on through the decades it developed millions of new little fans. In 1967, *Time* called *The Wizard* "the most popular single film property in the history of U.S. television." (In its earlier yearly run on CBS, when fewer homes had color sets, the movie had on at least one occasion been aired in black-and-white, making Oz look like a fizzier Kansas.) It continued to seduce home viewers on VHS and laser disc, DVD and Blu-ray. A 75th Anniversary Collector's Edition offers the movie in 3-D, stirring two quick reactions: Wow! and Why?

It is a great movie, as we have said, and it is also an important movie, precisely *because* it is much more than its bells and whistles. Behind the intense and durable entertainment value of this ultimate studio production, *The Wizard of Oz* matters because it speaks in subtext to so many segments of its audience. It is fun and exciting and even

glorious, certainly. But it is, underneath, a multiple act of empowerment for traditionally powerless groups.

We'll try in this next little bit to briefly analyze four aspects of the film without strangling all the fun out of the movie. Then we'll return to the pure fun.

KID POWER

Here's how a child might see the movie's plot: An orphan girl lives—subsists, actually—on a Kansas farm surrounded by stern, oafish, duplicitous or downright mean adults. Em, the woman who runs the place, radiates all the grace of a prison matron while bossing her weaker husband, Henry, and her three feckless farmhands. With no friends her own age, Dorothy must confide her dreams of a land over the rainbow to her dog, Toto. But now a truly evil adult, Miss Gulch, gets a sheriff's order to have Toto totaled—which sends sobs like stabs through the girl's heart. To protect her pet, Dorothy runs away from home. On the road she meets Professor Marvel, who falsely hints that her aunt is dying. Her niecely responsibility trumping all hope of escape, she returns home, where a tornado whisks her out of Kansas and, voilà, into a Technicolor land of sunshine, lollipops and rainbows. Also: wicked witches, flying monkeys and narcotic poppies. Still, the place is less like a sentence than an exclamation point. Free at last!

This *Wizard* movie differed from other, earlier children's films in several ways. The earliest Disney animated features, for example, painted childhood as an unrelenting nightmare, from which the young protagonists eventually escaped to a happy ending more by luck than by heroism. The Disney portrayal of childhood misery allowed kids to see Pinocchio's or Dumbo's plights as extreme cases from which children could distance themselves; their lives weren't *that* bad.

But Dorothy's life on the farm: It wasn't tragic, just dull and painful, like a toothache with no dentist in

---

*This is the **Majestic Theatre*** at the corner of Columbus Circle and 59th Street in Manhattan—today, right where the Time Warner Center sits at the southwest corner of Central Park—with the theatrical* Wizard of Oz *on the marquee. The year is 1903. This stage production let everyone know they were right:* The Wizard *could be reinterpreted.*

THE MUSEUM OF THE CITY OF NEW YORK/ART RESOURCE, NY

sight. In other words, the recognizable existence of a lonely kid. And Oz, for all its mortal hazards, offered Dorothy an adventure through which she could reveal the ove and nobility that no one thought to ask her to display at home.

Many other classic children's fables painted life as surrealistic, a dreamscape for the underage protagonist to wander through. Lewis Carroll's Alice, a wonderland girl who bowed 35 years before Baum published his first *Oz* book, observed the frantic charades of the Mad Hatter and the March Hare with a bemused passivity. Dorothy, by contrast, was an activist: at first by default, when her house crushes the Wicked Witch of the West's sister, and then by defying death in her crusade to find the Wizard and somehow earn her passage back home. The crafty malevolence of the Wicked Witch, the fuming and stalling of the Wizard, the winsome incompetence of the Scarecrow, Tin Man and Lion—none of these can derail Dorothy's commitment to her quest. Let adults be corseted by convention and compromise; this girl has more brains, heart, courage and wisdom than all the grown-ups. A little child shall lead them.

At first, MGM took that Isaiah quote literally: The studio brass hoped to borrow Shirley Temple, then nine years old and the biggest star at 20th Century Fox, to play Dorothy. In retrospect, the idea seems daft. Temple, for all her skills, would be no match for Dorothy's adult adversaries. She can't charm them, which was Temple's strategy in her Fox films. She must defy and defeat them. And how could that chipper moppet have ever located the hope and ache with which Garland invested "Over the Rainbow"? MGM's awarding of the role to the 16-year-old Judy proved to be one of Hollywood's smartest, luckiest casting choices, up there with Jack Warner's decision to replace Ronald Reagan with Humphrey Bogart as Rick in *Casablanca*. Here's looking at you, Judy.

WOMAN POWER

Was L. Frank Baum a feminist, at a time when black males had become legally free to cast a vote but women of any color had not? He was indeed. As Meghan O'Rourke noted in a 2009 *Slate* essay, "Baum, who publicly supported women's right to vote, was deeply affected by his beloved, spirited wife, Maud, and her mother, Matilda [Gage], an eminent feminist who collaborated with Susan B. Anthony and publicized the idea that many 'witches' were really freethinking women ahead of their time. In *Oz* (the book), Baum offers a similarly corrective vision: When Dorothy first meets a witch, the Witch of the North, she says, 'I thought all witches were wicked.' 'Oh, no, that is a great mistake,' replies the Witch of the North." O'Rourke added, "In sequels, Oz's true ruler . . . turns out to be a girl named Ozma, who spent her youth under a spell—one that turned her into a hapless boy." The Wizard is just a regent; this empire has a Queen.

Baum's biographical details aside (we will investigate them shortly), the Oz of the original novel and the MGM movie, too, is a full-fledged matriarchy. On the Gale farm, the strongest figure is Auntie Em. In Oz, Glinda the Good Witch presides over Munchkinland. The Wicked Witch of the West is the Castro and the Che of her insurgent campaign—the usurping politician and the crafty military commander, lording it over the monkeys and the male guards. Opposing her is young Dorothy, devising schemes to infiltrate the Wicked Witch's castle and eventually killing her, while acting as the efficient surrogate mother of her three woebegone friends. Yes, the Wizard is the grand vizier and the ultimate granter of all fervent wishes, but the reign of the movie's one "strong" man is a ruse. And at the end he abdicates, floating off in a balloon, leaving a flummoxed Dorothy in charge (with the Scarecrow, the Tin Man and the Lion as her cabinet). If the homesick girl hadn't clicked her heels, she'd still be the Wizardess, waiting for Ozma.

Not very many American works of art translated into international successes in the 19th century, and The Wizard of Oz *was one of the first in the 20th century that started really changing the game. Larry Semon's 1925 film was, as we will learn, hardly great—but it was a commercial success and was one of the silent-era items that let the world know that Hollywood was coming.*

EVERETT

Gone with the Wind, MGM's other big 1939 film, was also predominantly a woman's movie, with Scarlett, Melanie and Mammy fighting to sustain their home and tend the children. But sexy Clark Gable tipped the scales toward a gender balance in that movie. In *The Wizard of Oz,* the males are all bumbling or bogus. The women of Oz perform all the magic, for good and ill. And one of them, a young stranger, saves the kingdom.

PROLETARIAN POWER

Virtually every adventure story includes a rebellion of the underdog against the ruling class; few movies find the 1 percent wonderful. Knowing that the poor filled more theater seats than the rich, particularly in 1939, the makers of *The Wizard of Oz* made its chief villain a wealthy landowner. Miss Gulch is not only a "sour-faced old maid," in the words of Hickory (later, the Tin Man), she is also the richest person in her part of Kansas. The film opens with Dorothy rushing urgently home after an (unseen) encounter with Gulch, who has whacked Toto after the dog toyed with her cat. Soon Gulch cycles over to the Gale farm with a sheriff's order for Toto's apprehension and demise, which prompts Auntie Em to uncork a little of Ma Joad's vinegar from *The Grapes of Wrath*: "Just because you own half the county doesn't mean you have the power to run the rest of us!" Oh, yes, she does, because, in this Kansas, money talks (Gulch had presumably exerted her financial and political influence to secure the order). The spiteful spinster essentially dognaps Toto—an act that triggers Dorothy's escape, and possibly the wrath of the tornado that lands her in Oz, where Gulch has morphed into the Wicked Witch of the West.

We've said that Auntie Em, Uncle Henry and the three farmhands—Dorothy's ostensible authority figures—provide her little parental love and guidance. She must find those qualities in Oz. Glinda has them in abundance, but she's not around much, appearing and disappearing at whim in a floating soap bubble. The Scarecrow, Tin Man and Cowardly Lion are Dorothy's boon companions but also her emotional dependents; *she* must pick *them* up. Nor can she trust Oz's supreme authority, the Wizard, who uses her as a one-girl counterrevolution, sending her on a suicide mission to steal the Wicked Witch's broomstick. Besides, as we learn, the "Great and Powerful Oz" is a fraud. So the meek—Dorothy—must not inherit the earth but seize it. Grave peril forces a common farm girl to find the unique heroism inside her. Back in Kansas, Dorothy didn't think of herself as extraordinary, only lonely and frustrated; her intuitive reaction to danger was flight. But now, finally, she learns to fight, in a new land whose threats don't sap her but give her strength. That was the movie's mixed message to its Depression-era audience: You can fulfill your fantasies by standing up for your rights. But to get to the finish line, you have to move. Leave the barren Great Plains! Crawl out of that Dust Bowl! Find the American Dream in the Oz of California and the Emerald City of Hollywood.

GAY POWER

Another group to whom *The Wizard of Oz* spoke, at least in semaphore, was homosexual men. In the decades before gay liberation, when their sexual activities were deemed crimes in America, they took heart in the movie's tale of people cloistered and repressed in drab Kansas who reveal their full eccentric glory in Technicolor Oz. Dorothy is transformed from a lonely child into the Munchkins' savior princess, and the farmhands into the Scarecrow, Tin Man and Cowardly Lion.

The three amigos of Oz are not exactly the Fellowship of the Ring. Comic relief as much as staunch warriors, they lack, respectively, a brain, a heart and "the noive." All are clinically reliant on Dorothy and easily intimidated—especially the Lion, who confesses, with mincing gestures

---

The Wizard *would prove to be a master of all media.* *In the mid-1930s, Nancy Kelly, not yet a teen, and Bill Adams (as the Scarecrow) perform a radio version of the story. The show is heard on the NBC network in 15-minute segments three times a week, and is sponsored by Jell-O gelatin. Very wholesome.*

EVERETT

and a toss of his blond curls, "Yeah, it's sad, believe me, Missy, / When you're born to be a sissy," and "I'm afraid there's no denyin' / I'm just a *dandy* lion." Yet Dorothy proclaims them "the best friends anybody ever had" (perhaps because her only previous friend couldn't talk, only bark). These pals of Dorothy come "out" on the Yellow Brick Road to help her search for the godlike Wizard. Plus they get to sing and dance. They could be the Emerald City's Village People.

Not long after the film's release, gays began employing the phrase "Friend of Dorothy" as a code for introducing themselves to other men without risking assault, arrest or blackmail. The name stuck; a half-century later, cruise-ship schedules would announce meetings for Friends of Dorothy, or FOD, as a delicate way of saying, without frightening the straights on board, that gays were welcome to socialize. But not everyone was savvy about the acronym. In his 1994 book, *Conduct Unbecoming: Gays & Lesbians in the U.S. Military*, Randy Shilts reported that around 1980 the Naval Investigative Service, unaware of the phrase's meaning, "believed that a woman named Dorothy was the hub of an enormous ring of military homosexuals . . . [They] prepared to hunt Dorothy down and convince her to give them the names of homosexuals." Aside from its hilarious and malign cluelessness, this Dorothy caper makes the definitive argument for allowing gays all equality in the military—at least in the NIS.

As we know, when Garland aged from sweet teen to tragic diva, before her death at 47 in 1969, gays embraced her as their den mother and the MGM film as their story. John Waters, onetime naughty filmmaker (*Pink Flamingos*) and the all-time Cardinal of Camp—the Dandy Lion of directors—has given this lavender précis of the movie's plot: "Girl leaves drab farm, becomes a fag hag, meets gay lions and men that don't try to molest her, and meets a witch, kills her. And unfortunately—by a surreal act of shoe fetishism—clicks her shoes together and is back to where she belongs. It has an unhappy ending." Waters knew, as we all do, that Dorothy and her Friends belonged not in Kansas but in Oz; that's where they can flounce and flourish. And speaking of shoe fetishism: In 2005, when one of the few surviving pairs of ruby slippers was stolen from Garland's childhood home in Grand Rapids, Minnesota (reborn as the Judy Garland Museum), David Letterman deadpanned that "the thief is described as 'armed and fabulous.'"

Enough deep think? Yes, maybe enough. But it's all fun to consider. So too are the circumstances of how this miraculous movie came together—the hits and near misses, beyond Garland's casting, that allowed *The Wizard of Oz* to become a near-perfect picture.

As you will learn in our pages, so much that is now regarded as great and just right was accidental or backup. Let's look at the music, for a starter. Everyone might admit the music is a highlight of *The Wizard of Oz*. But how did it happen?

Arthur Freed had wanted Jerome Kern, the dean of American composers, to write the music for *The Wizard*'s songs, but Kern had been weakened by a recent heart attack and was unavailable. MGM considered two songwriting duos (Harry Revel and Mack Gordon, and Nacio Herb Brown and Al Dubin) before settling on Harold Arlen and Yip Harburg. The son of a Buffalo, New York, cantor, Arlen had written a slew of hits—"Get Happy," "Between the Devil and the Deep Blue Sea," "I Love a Parade," "I Gotta Right to Sing the Blues," "I've Got the World on a String," "Happy as the Day Is Long," "Stormy Weather" and "Let's Fall in Love"—all with lyricist Ted Koehler. He began teaming with Harburg in 1932 for the Broadway revue *Americana*.

Judy Garland reads the holy text with Baum's widow, Maud, a feminist and daughter of the noted suffragist and freethinker Matilda Joslyn Gage. Maud's views were shared by her husband, Frank, and he certainly infused The Wizard of Oz *with a modern way of thinking. Gregory Maguire much later took this forward in* Wicked, *and his story is something of a feminist anthem.*

EVERETT

Like Kern, Irving Berlin and Cole Porter before them, Arlen and Harburg had gone West to write for movies. The money was good, the audience huge; all the songwriters lacked was the authority they enjoyed on Broadway, where they decided which songs went into a show. In Hollywood, where the producers were in charge, most movie musicals contained only five or six songs, instead of the dozen or more in a typical Broadway show.

The Wizard of Oz would be different. It's a full score of eight pieces, some divided into sections, like the elaborate Munchkinland musical sequence (for which Arlen composed seven discrete themes) and the three "If I Only Had a Heart/a Brain/the Nerve" solos. Elegantly constructed, yet hummable by any child, these numbers drive the narrative rather than simply ornament it. (Virtually all the songs are introduced in the movie's first half. When the melodrama kicks in as Dorothy petitions the Wizard and confronts the Wicked Witch, the characters stop singing.)

Identified with the bluesy numbers he wrote for Ethel Waters and Cab Calloway at Harlem's Cotton Club, Arlen didn't approach this adaptation of a children's book by writing down to the kiddies. Most songs are in a major key, and the jazz inflections are muted—the score's one up-tempo bluesy number, "The Jitterbug," was cut during production, and we'll read about that later—but Arlen's melodies are as intricate as ever. Harburg had free rein to exercise his lyrical wit in pinwheeling wordplay for the Munchkins and the Scarecrow, Tin Man and Lion. The song cycle in the early Oz scenes is musical storytelling of the highest, most effervescent order: Glinda's "Come Out, Come Out, Wherever You Are," Dorothy's "The House Began to Pitch" (for which Harburg confected 10 "witch" rhymes), the Munchkin Mayor and Coroner numbers, the Lullaby League and Lollipop Guild trios, "We Welcome You to Munchkinland" and the celebratory "Ding-Dong! The Witch Is Dead." (Just by the way: Songs for the Wizard and the Wicked Witch of the West were considered but never written.)

Freed and Arlen agreed on the need for a ballad that would connect Dorothy's confinement in Kansas with the wonders she meets in Oz. In an April 1938 memo outlining his thoughts on the project, Freed had noted how, in Disney's *Snow White,* "the whole love story . . . is motivated by the song 'Some Day My Prince Will Come.'" He suggested an early "musical sequence on the farm" that would express a similar longing. This was the challenge: a ballad without romance—less a love song than a prayer.

One day, as his wife, Anya, was driving him through Los Angeles, Arlen asked her to pull over in front of Schwab's drugstore. With the car idling, he jotted down a musical idea that would become "Over the Rainbow." Talk about dramatic: There's a full-octave jump from the first note ("Some-") to the second ("-where"), instantly expressing a vaulting emotion and establishing Dorothy as a woman (lower octave) who is also a girl (upper octave). Later he added a bridge ("Someday I'll wish upon a star") of alternating notes, as in a child's piano exercise, to be sung "dreamily." Simple yet sophisticated, the tune seemed a gift from above. As Arlen later recalled, "It was as if the Lord said, 'Well, here it is. Now stop worrying about it.'"

His worries had just begun. First, Harburg resisted the idea; he wanted the patter songs to carry the story, and he hated the opening octave jump. Ira Gershwin had to persuade Harburg of the melody's merit, and only then Harburg set to work. He reasoned that in Dorothy's Kansas, "an arid place where not even flowers grow, her only familiarity with colors would have been the sight of a rainbow." After trying to drop those first two notes, he hit on the "Somewhere" that today seems perfect and inevitable. See? All perfect, but so happenstance.

Gershwin suggested the song's kicker, which repeats the first two musical phrases of the bridge ("If happy little bluebirds fly / Beyond the rainbow . . ."), then soars into ethereal yearning ("Why, oh why, can't I?").

It is a superb song.

The big guns at MGM thought it was disposable. Incredible, but true. Arlen and Freed had to overcome the resistance of the studio bosses, who balked at filming the segment and then cut the song three times during the editing process. As late as a sneak preview in Pomona, California, on June 16, 1939, barely two months before the August premiere, "Over the

BISON ARCHIVES

It is said that Grauman's Chinese Theatre, *which opened in the later 1920s, has been the site of more big-time Hollywood premieres than any other movie house. In 1939 it certainly is the focus of the frenzy as 10,000 Southern Californians form a crush for the Hollywood bow of MGM's* The Wizard of Oz.

Rainbow" was not in the movie. Also true.

We posit the usual explanations in our pages—it was too slow; it was too sophisticated for the kids—but really: What were they thinking, and how did *The Wizard of Oz* dodge some of these bullets, while hitting bull's-eye after bull's-eye with others?

It can be supposed that, vis-à-vis "Over the Rainbow," one possible explanation for the moguls' skepticism was that Garland, in her early films at MGM, had made her rep less as a balladeer than as a jive singer and comedienne, with such numbers as "Swing, Mr. Mendelssohn, Swing" and "Zing! Went the Strings of My Heart." In her solo movie debut, the 1936 short *Every Sunday*, Judy sings the jazzy "Waltz with a Swing" while her young costar, Deanna Durbin, performs the operatic "Il Bacio." (Some MGM solons wanted Durbin as Dorothy.) Garland's little-girl looks contrasted almost freakishly with her precociously mature contralto and knowing way with a lyric. In the Roger Edens song "In-Between," from the 1938 *Love Finds Andy Hardy*, she addresses her awkward adolescence in words that prefigure Dorothy's restlessness on the Gale farm: "I'm not a child, / All children bore me. / I'm not grown-up, / Grown-ups ignore me."

Of course, we now know: It is precisely Garland's "in-between" status as a grown-up child that helped make her rendition of "Over the Rainbow" so powerful.

She was originally to sing it to Auntie Em and the farmhands. When Fleming left to direct *Gone with the Wind*, King Vidor—who had directed the populist films *Hallelujah!* and *Our Daily Bread*, both set on farms— took over the shooting of the Kansas material, and it was Vidor who purified the number into a votive secret that Dorothy shares with her only friend, Toto, and with the movie audience. Filmed in just a few shots, and pristinely performed by an unblinking Judy, it is the scene that displays the film's first and lasting moments of magic—not of wit or color or special effects, but of the ideal fusion of music and lyric, situation and singer. And emotion. Every listener touched by this song should think of Harold Arlen on that corner in front of Schwab's and join him in saying, "Thank you, Lord."

That song—and the music generally—is presented as one of the earlier miracles. There would be many more, including the final fate of the movie itself.

The Wizard of Oz always relied on special effects, but it could not and would not be significant 75 years later if its greatness were *due to* special effects. It relied on Oz, yes, but it relied as well on Kansas.

Here we'll return to some probing, if you don't mind—because *The Wizard of Oz* is sturdy enough to stand it.

National heroine, legendary warrior, Empress for life toward the movie's end: What else could Dorothy want? She says she wants Kansas—that monochromatic land where no one shows her love and a mean lady takes Toto away to be killed. To justify Dorothy's decision to return from Oz to the Gale farm, the screenwriters attempted an impossible headstand and fell flat on their prats. In Dorothy's big speech about the lesson she's learned, she tells Glinda: "If I ever go looking for my heart's desire again, I won't look any further than my own backyard. Because if it isn't there, I never really lost it to begin with." She adds, "Is that right?"— as if seeking validation for the gibberish she has just spouted. And Glinda, like an indulgent schoolteacher trying to encourage a sweet if slightly backward third-grader, smilingly confirms, "That's all it is!"

But what is it? Back in Kansas, Dorothy had boldly expressed her heart's desire—indeed, she sang it—in her very own backyard. For the girl to return to the status quo, minus the urge to escape its stultifying restrictions, would

---

This is a "jumbo window card" issued during the film's release in 1939. It is interesting for various reasons. First, it broadcasts MGM's aspiration and paranoia as it competes with Disney, and so desperately hopes to equal Snow White. *And then, with Morgan and Haley and Bolger and Lahr and Grapewin, it seems a leaflet for vaudeville.*

EVERETT

almost be a lobotomy of the soul. (The tone is even darker in Disney's *Return to Oz,* where Auntie Em wants Dorothy to get electroshock therapy.) And yet she clicks her heels, summons the words of John Howard Payne's 1823 lyric and says, "There's no place like home." She wakens in bed, with Auntie Em, Uncle Henry, the farmhands and Professor Marvel stirred to sympathy by the bump on the head she got during the cyclone. Actually, her "home"—the Gale house—is the instrument that propelled Dorothy to Oz. In that sense, she never left it to begin with.

In the Baum book, Dorothy explains her homesickness this way: "No matter how dreary and gray our homes are, we people of flesh and blood would rather live there than in any other country, be it ever so beautiful. There is no place like home." Thus she acknowledges the lure of faraway places while affirming that her emotional compass always points homeward. In the movie, Dorothy articulates little of that nuance. From what we've seen of her Kansas, there's no place like home for drudgery and boredom; she's like a lifer who wishes she were back in her cell. Would the Joads look back to the parched land they left and croon, "There's no place like Oklahoma"? How're ya gonna keep 'em down on the farm after they've seen the Emerald City?

For the movie to propel Dorothy and the viewer willingly back home, Kansas must have something Oz doesn't. Producer Arthur Freed thought he knew the answer: an orphan girl's love for her surrogate mother. In his April 1938 memo, he described Dorothy as a girl "who finds herself with a heart full of love eager to give it, but through circumstances and personalities, can apparently find none in return. In this dilemma of childish frustration, she is hit on the head in a real cyclone and through her unconscious self, she finds escape in her dream of Oz. There she is motivated by her generosity to help everyone first before her little orphan heart cries out for what she wants most of all (the love of Aunt Em)—which represents to her the love of a mother she never knew."

Freed's memo brandishes some acute psychology—and proof that he knew from the start that this would be more than a kid-centric fantasy musical—that is not necessarily evident in the movie. First, the film makes no allusion to Dorothy's real mother (or father); her orphan status must be a condition she long ago accepted. And second, as played by Clara Blandick, Auntie Em is a bitter pill. Stern of demeanor, she is seen smiling only twice: once in a photo Dorothy carries (and the Professor borrows) and once at the end, when Dorothy "comes home." To Em, in her preoccupation with counting chickens, her niece is little more than a barnyard critter under her feet. Heedless of Dorothy's pleas about Miss Gulch's intent to abduct and kill Toto, Em admonishes her to go "find yourself a place where you won't get into any trouble." That's when Dorothy sings "Over the Rainbow," a dream not of maternal love but of freedom from Auntie Em and the rest of Kansas.

We know that many of the Kansans—Miss Gulch, Professor Marvel and the three farmhands—reappear in Dorothy's dream of Oz. The one Oz character who could be wholly the figment of her imagination is Glinda. Wise, capable and still as gorgeous as a Ziegfeld girl (Burke, who turned 54 the month the movie opened, was Florenz Ziegfeld's widow), Glinda is a good—no, a great—witch, and the perfect fairy godmother for a lonely child who hopes against hope for a sympathetic maternal figure. (Could Glinda be the Auntie Em of Oz? Not likely. If the movie's creators thought so, they would have cast the same actress in both roles. They thought about it, and wisely decided against.) Glinda materializes and vanishes magically, like the sainted mother in the tenderest dreams of any orphan. Much later, Harry Potter would have such visitations from the mother he never knew. Back in Kansas, Dorothy must make do with the aunt who rarely smiles. Or maybe the adults will treat her more kindly now, since she may have been in a coma "for days and days." That's where we are left, and we wonder.

Dorothy may never escape Kansas, but moviegoers can always return to Oz. Of all the estimable movies from Hollywood's Golden Age, *The Wizard of Oz* is the one that has never gone out of fashion. It requires no apologies for anachronistic views on race, as *Gone with the Wind* does.

EVERETT

Modern viewers, whose main complaints about old movies are that they are too dark and too slow, needn't adjust their eyes and clocks to *The Wizard*. Once Dorothy alights in Munchkinland, the film bursts into riotous color and zips along like a Pixar cartoon epic—but with songs, great songs, the very best songs. The songs are for the ages, and so, finally and even with flaws, is the story. *The Wizard of Oz*'s enveloping fantasy world allows for no contemporary references that would be obscure today.

Timeless then, it is timeless now. Ask yourself: Who isn't eager, at any moment, to soar with Dorothy over the rainbow and into the Merry Old Land of Oz?

In a lobby card trumpeting a rerelease, the 1939 film that will live forevermore is promoted. Probably more than any other great work of art, The Wizard of Oz *is half one thing and half the other. It is the book and the movie. The film is an interpretation, yes. But it is perfectly itself.*

DANA HALL/EVERETT

Who was L. FRANK BAUM?

Like his greatest creation, he was sweet, fanciful and
quite a piece of work. Having practiced his storytelling on
four sons, he found his métier and renown in his forties.
Thereafter, he, more than anyone, *was* the Wizard of Oz.
*Opposite: A studio portrait made
in 1908, by which time Baum was known as an
"author, actor and soon-to-be filmmaker."*

Born in 1856 smack-dab in the middle of New York State in a village called Chittenango, which today hosts an annual Oz-Stravaganza Festival, Lyman Frank Baum enjoyed many things about his upbringing—with a few marked exceptions. He didn't like his first name, which had been bequeathed from an uncle, and so when he came around to fashioning a byline, "Lyman" became simply "L." And he didn't much enjoy his time at the Peekskill Military Academy, where he was sent at age 12 and lasted two years, and so when he came around to writing his most famous book he satirized the authoritarian regimen he had encountered via the Wicked Witch's troops, including her squadron of monkeys.

Frank Baum was by all accounts a friendly and fanciful boy and young man who kept drifting from this dream to that one. On a printing press that he owned he published an amateur newspaper, *The Rose Lawn Home Journal,* and later hand-set the type for a privately printed collection of his poems: *By the Candelabra's Glare: Some Verse.* He edited *The Aberdeen Saturday Pioneer,* a weekly journal, and tried his hand at store ownership, but Baum's Bazaar was a bust.

He married Maud Gage in 1882, and together they would build a family of four sons. Frank, a gentle-hearted man, could never bring himself to discipline the boys. The real child-rearing was left to Maud, although the father did entertain

— ◆ —

Looking wizardly in the middle is the author himself, surrounded by several of his Oz-ian children during a 1908 Fairylogue and Radio-Plays *stage show and movie that he produced (and wished he hadn't).*

WRITER PICTURES/AP

his children with fantastic, dramatically rendered storytelling.

He had a penchant for it, of that there's no doubt. His first large success as a writer (and incidentally as an actor) came in the year of his marriage when, as Louis F. Baum, he wrote the melodramatic play (with songs) *The Maid of Arran, an Idyllic Irish Drama Written for the People, Irrespective of Caste or Nationality* (described additionally as "A Play to Ensnare All Hearts and Leave an Impress of Beauty and Nobility Within the Sordid Mind of Man"). Baum played the lead role on tour (with a stop in Kansas, the only time he ever visited the state) and during two separate New York engagements.

But, with the exception of his family life, he couldn't settle down and he struggled to find his niche; fame and fortune were elusive. Then, in 1897, as he was entering his forties, he published *Mother Goose in Prose,* with illustrations by the great Maxfield Parrish. Two years later his *Father Goose, His Book,* illustrated by W.W. Denslow, was the year's best-selling picture book. In the introduction to his and Denslow's 1900 follow-up, Baum declared his intentions: "*The Wonderful Wizard of Oz* was written solely to please children of today. It aspires to be a modernized fairy tale, in which the wonderment and joy are retained and the heart-aches and nightmares are left out."

Well, not all the nightmares had been

CHICAGO HISTORY MUSEUM/UIG/GETTY

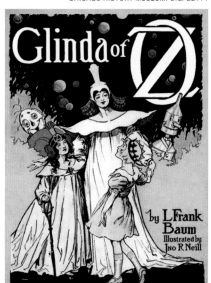

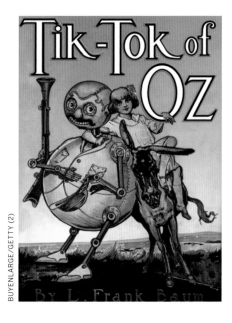

BUYENLARGE/GETTY (2)

left out, but the novel brought pleasure to children in its day, and has continued to ever since.

Baum was now a huge literary figure, and the way he lived the remaining two decades of his life—he would die on May 6, 1919, at age 62, in Hollywood, California, several months after gallbladder surgery—tells us that, perhaps, he should have stuck to the literary side of it. He wrote 13 more novels set in Oz, many of them very successful and the whole of them, taken together, became the underpinning of a series of sequels that continued after his death, not to mention a cottage industry of other properties, from movies to newer plays to plush dolls. He published some 60 novels, many under pseudonyms, from Floyd Akers to Laura Bancroft to Edith Van Dyne, and also penned scores of short stories, poems and plays.

But, restless beyond accounting, he continued to dabble in the theater and then the film industry, usually with his *Oz* material, and that dabbling is not his legacy, nor was it cause for great pleasure. He fell out with his illustrator, Denslow, over theatrical royalties; his film company was about as successful as Baum's Bazaar had been.

He had long suffered from a weak heart and was ill when he died. But to the end he would write while sitting up in bed. There, with paper and pen, L. Frank Baum was in the Emerald City. What a place to be.

◆

Down the decades, the Oz backlist burgeoned and so did its audience (opposite, at the Miller Colony in Montana in 1968, a Hutterite girl is transfixed by a reprint of the original novel). Above, from top: A poster by Oz's original illustrator, W.W. Denslow, then book jackets from two of the subsequent 13 Oz books written by Baum.

TED STRESHINSKY/CORBIS

Baum was theatrical, his story was theatrical, and almost before the ink was dry on a second printing of *The Wonderful Wizard of Oz*, there were theatrical productions and soon movies (the early films were what are now called "shorts"). The 1902 musical, which was vastly reworked from a 1901 operetta, featuring a doctored script and some lyrics by Baum, costumes and sets by Denslow and music by a tunesmith named A. Baldwin Sloane and a classically oriented young Missourian named Paul Tietjens, was one of the great stage successes in the early years of the 20th century, and sent *The Wizard* down the paved-with-gold road as an eternally popular vehicle. According to Baum, "The thought of making my fairy tale into a play had never even occurred to me when, one evening, my doorbell rang and I found a spectacled young man standing on the mat." This would have been Tietjens, under the spell of Baum's wizardry, importuning the great man to allow an adaptation. It is an account approximately as fanciful as flying monkeys. More prosaic and probably accurate reports have an agent introducing Baum and Tietjens, or Denslow twisting Baum's arm and insisting something along the lines of, "Good God, man! This was *made* for the stage!"

And so it *was* made for the stage, which Baum certainly never regretted. Further plays, musicals and movies were fashioned (including a famous moving-picture production, seen at left). In recent years there have been ballets, cartoons and all the rest. But the point is: *Oz* left the page for the stage as if propelled by a Kansas tornado.

———— ◆ ————

In 1925, the writer, director and actor Larry Semon (here, as Scarecrow) made a silent film in which he was top-billed over Dorothy Dwan (center) and a comic actor who would enjoy a longer-lasting film career: That's Oliver Hardy, Stan Laurel's partner, dressed in Tinseltown tin.

EVERETT

The first musical, *produced by Fred R. Hamlin, debuted at the Grand Opera House in Chicago on June 16, 1902, then toured for a bit and opened at the marvelous new Majestic Theatre on Columbus Circle in New York City on January 21, 1903; the scenes on these pages were recorded at the Majestic, and that's Toto's substitute, Imogene, being admonished by Dorothy. The showbiz story goes that Hamlin risked his dough on this show because his family had made a pile with Hamlin's Wizard Oil, a cure-all elixir. His investment paid off in spades as the musical toured throughout the decade and even became a 13-minute silent film in 1910 featuring an all-girl production number and a scene with the Woodman playing a piccolo—and, of course, including Imogene.*

THE MUSEUM OF THE CITY OF NEW YORK/ART RESOURCE, NY (3)

EVERETT (2)

The Oz film manufacturing *company got up and running in 1914 with* The Patchwork Girl of Oz, *followed by* The Magic Cloak of Oz *and then* His Majesty, the Scarecrow of Oz *(opposite, Frank Moore as the Scarecrow; above, French acrobat Pierre Couderc—remembered by cineasts—as the Tin Man). Baum was intimately involved in this effort to form one of the first movie studios in Hollywood, though he invested little of his own money, having been burned by his financial involvement in the earlier* Fairylogue *and* Radio-Plays *productions. The first movie in particular was well received critically, but these new Oz films fared poorly at the box office, and the studio shuttered quickly.*

CHADWICK PICTURES/KOBAL/ART RESOURCE, NY
ENTERTAINMENT PICTURES/ZUMA

Larry Semon's 1925 *movie version still left lots of room for MGM—or someone—to revisit the magical source material. Opposite: Semon with Dorothy Dwan as the fictional Dorothy. Above: Dorothy in Oz.*

ENTERTAINMENT PICTURES/ZUMA

Silly slapstick *scenes and racist stereotyping make Larry Semon's version of* The Wizard of Oz *unwatchable today, despite Oliver Hardy's presence (right, at far right). Semon (featured here in all three photos) worked often with Hardy—coincidentally, he had also worked with Stan Laurel, Hardy's soon-to-be sidekick—and at one point was considered a comic star of near-Chaplin stature. But this film put his reputation, and consequently his career, into eclipse.*

CHADWICK PICTURES/PHOTOFEST

EVERETT

Grand finales were yet to come in the Wizard of Oz saga, but this was director Larry Semon's in 1925. He had been a cartoonist, and so was drawn to the imaginary and also the impossible—special effects, exploding barns, falling water towers. Big, big, big. In this way, he was a perfect early big-screen interpreter of The Wizard of Oz. He had been hugely successful as a comic in the one-reel era, but overreached, got himself into financial trouble and then dove headlong into feature films like The Wizard of Oz in hopes of finding a way out. By 1927, he had retreated to short subjects. The next year he filed for bankruptcy. He then returned to vaudeville, but suffered a nervous breakdown. He checked into the sanatorium in Victorville, California. He was only 39 when he died on October 8, 1928. Semon remains an important, if sad, side-story in the history of The Wizard of Oz.

CHADWICK PICTURES/PHOTOFEST

Sowing the
SEEDS

The so-called golden age of the Metro-Goldwyn-Mayer musical commenced in the post–World War II years, when the studio boasted "more stars than there are in heaven." But an early MGM salvo was with *The Wizard of Oz,* when execs couldn't even decide who their stars might be. Here's a pictorial history of the film coming together.
Opposite: Veteran hoofer Ray Bolger, in a makeup test for the role he would play, was originally supposed to be the Tin Man. The guy who would later become TV's Jed Clampett was supposed to be the Scarecrow. All will be explained in the pages that follow.

BISON ARCHIVES

As Richard Corliss writes in his introductory essay for this book, not only wasn't this movie a sure thing for the longest time, many things about it—starting with who would play Dorothy—weren't sure things until the cameras were actually rolling. Five directors would work on the movie; four of them, including Hollywood legends King Vidor and George Cukor, uncredited. Among an even larger list of uncredited script writers were such as Ogden Nash and Herman J. Mankiewicz. A lot of talent, certainly: But when the credits and noncredits of any film project extend to this length and become a mishmash, that's usually a recipe for disaster. That the movie got made at all seems, in retrospect, marvelous: a fortuitous delight. That *The Wizard of Oz* became one of the greatest movies ever made seems miraculous.

In the pages that follow, we present pictures—many of them behind the scenes, some of them intimate, a few rarely if ever seen—that show how the movie came together: *The Wizard of Oz* when the seeds were being sown. The movie stills to follow in our next chapter are resonant in that they bring us back to the film, and our personal memories. But first: This is different stuff that we don't remember, and perhaps have never seen the like of.

What? You haven't witnessed a tree being directed? Well, maybe you have, if there is such a shot of Peter Jackson during the filming of *The Lord of the Rings: The Two Towers.* But if you're lacking in that experience, turn the page, and be delighted.

———————— •◆• ————————

***Producer Mervyn LeRoy,** in the dark suit, Judy Garland and director Victor Fleming pose with Munchkins on the set. LeRoy was, as well, one of the four uncredited directors. In the lead-up to the film's release, MGM promoted Garland, to be sure, but the story already had been disseminated that Shirley Temple had been preferred by many at the studio. The big news that film fans couldn't get enough of was about the Munchkins, a group of more than a hundred small performers put together by German vaudeville promoter Leo Singer. So MGM's public relations office focused its most intense efforts on them.*

MGM/PHOTOFEST

MGM/PHOTOFEST

EVERETT

Victor Fleming's job *was not an easy one. He had all these other directors looking over his shoulder, the great Vidor in charge of the Kansas scenes, and trees to deal with, as he does admirably opposite. Above, Fleming has a sit-down with Scarecrow Bolger, producer Mervyn LeRoy (at far right) and an unidentified man. On the job, Fleming is always dapper—always Hollywood. This would be his year—1939—with* The Wizard *and* Gone With the Wind, *for which he would win the Oscar.*

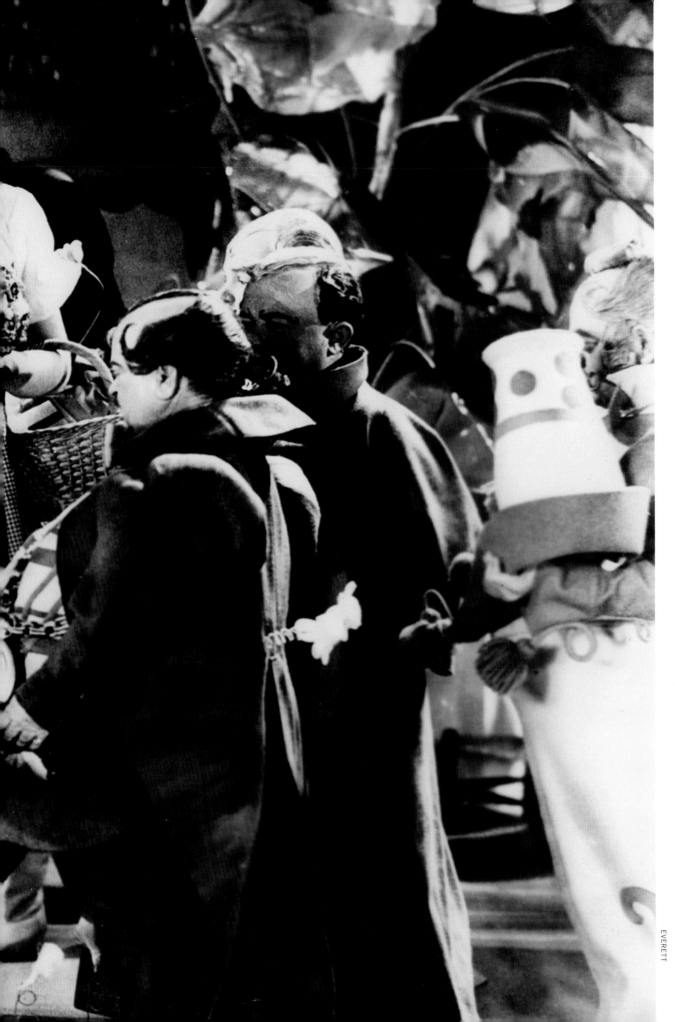

EVERETT

Fleming graciously directs the feisty Munchkins while Garland looks on. The dwarfishness of this brood in the film was largely an invention of the filmmakers. In the book, Baum described his denizens of Oz thusly, as first perceived by Dorothy: "[S]he noticed coming down toward her a group of the queerest people she had ever seen. They were not as big as the grown folk she had always been used to; but neither were they very small. In fact, they seemed about as tall as Dorothy, who was a well-grown child for her age, although they were, so far as looks go, many years older." So the filmic version isn't too far off, but these Oz-ians are uniformly smaller.

MGM/KOBAL/ART RESOURCE, NY

BISON ARCHIVES

MGM/PHOTOFEST

MGM/PHOTOFEST

Figuring it out *was a big part of the making of* The Wizard of Oz. *It was to be a musical, and so the estimable Herbert Stothart (opposite) had a job as the principal conductor and would win the Best Original Score Oscar for his captivating music. There was need for a Dorothy, of course, and so Judy Garland, most famous for her association with Mickey Rooney (top left, with MGM chief Louis B. Mayer), would ultimately have a job. There was need for a director, and so Fleming, top right, cutting the cake at his own birthday party with Garland, actress Myrna Loy (not in the film) and Frank Morgan (the Wizard), had a job. And there was need for Munchkins, and so scores of little people (seen above on the street outside the MGM studio in Culver City, California) had jobs.*

BISON ARCHIVES

HULTON/GETTY

The music! *The music was always imagined as a big part of the picture, but it emerged as one of the biggest parts ("Over the Rainbow" has topped many polls as the greatest Hollywood song ever). Above, we have in the back row, Bert Lahr, Ray Bolger, MGM exec L.K. Sidney, the movie's lyricist Yip Harburg, Meredith Willson (whose greatest fame as a music writer lies in* The Music Man*) and music publisher Harry Link; in the front row, Garland and the main man, songwriter Harold Arlen. Opposite: Judy Garland in the recording studio taping one of her tracks.*

ALLAN GRANT

Opposite: *Producer Mervyn LeRoy, doing double duty. Above, others who were involved: Director Norman Taurog, seen here with Jerry Lewis (left), won the Academy Award for* Skippy *in 1931 (the youngest ever to win the prize), worked with Rooney and Garland—and Spencer Tracy and Gene Kelly and Fred Astaire and even Elvis Presley—directed 180 films, and shot the tests for* Wizard. *Right: The man in the spectacles is King Vidor, directing James Murray and Eleanor Boardman in* The Crowd. Vidor, *not Victor Fleming, was responsible for* The Wizard's *sepia-toned "Kansas" scenes.*

JOHN SPRINGER COLLECTION/CORBIS

The cast! *What to say about the cast, except that MGM, despite itself, lucked out—big-time: The perfect cast (which we can all now admit* was *the perfect cast) wasn't for one second foreseen as the perfect cast. Certainly, Shirley Temple would have been fine and oh-so-cute as Dorothy, but would she have sung "Over the Rainbow" with such tender longing as Judy Garland did? Certainly, Buddy Ebsen would have been fine as the Scarecrow—maybe even the equal of Ray Bolger—but would that have left bandy-legged Bolger inside the tin suit, and if so would the Tin Man have been devoid of Jack Haley's innate, constant sweetness, so essential to one who felt he lacked a heart? Frank Morgan wasn't supposed to be the Wizard, either. If Bert Lahr was a likely lion from the get-go, he was the exception in a cast of constant fluxes. Some of what follows has been touched upon by Richard Corliss already, but needs to be reiterated and codified in the concise fashion that movie fans love. Therefore, here are the players, from left.*

Scarecrow: This was supposed to be Buddy Ebsen, a vaudeville veteran and genial second banana just like Ray Bolger. Ebsen would go on to greater fame as Jed Clampett in The Beverly Hillbillies. *Bolger was going to be the Tin Man. But Bolger desired to play the Scarecrow: "I'm not a tin performer, I'm fluid." This sentiment resonated with Ebsen, who willingly moved over to the Tin Man role, but then found himself allergic to chemicals used in the costume and makeup.*

Wizard: This was to be the great comedian W.C. Fields, and it could have been a career-defining role above his other career-defining roles. But he and MGM couldn't agree on a price, and the gig went to Morgan, and this certainly became Morgan's career-defining role.

Cowardly Lion: Bert Lahr was signed to portray the Cowardly Lion on July 25, 1938, and that's the most straightforward news here.

Tin Man: So Ebsen gallantly switched to the Tin Man role and then suffered a near-fatal reaction to the costume's aluminum-dust makeup. The makeup was switched to a paste, but that was it for Buddy, who was replaced by fellow vaudeville veteran Jack Haley— who also missed four days of shooting because the new makeup was less than perfect.

Dorothy: Producer Mervyn LeRoy was being leaned on to cast Shirley Temple, the world's most popular child star. Deanna Durbin was also a contender. In the event, the role fell to MGM player Garland. Temple's movie The Little Princess *outgrossed* The Wizard of Oz *in 1939, but that hardly matters today.*

And by the way: Margaret Hamilton was chosen as the Wicked Witch of the West just three days before filming began on October 13, 1938. She was not the first choice for the role either.

MGM/KOBAL/ART RESOURCE, NY

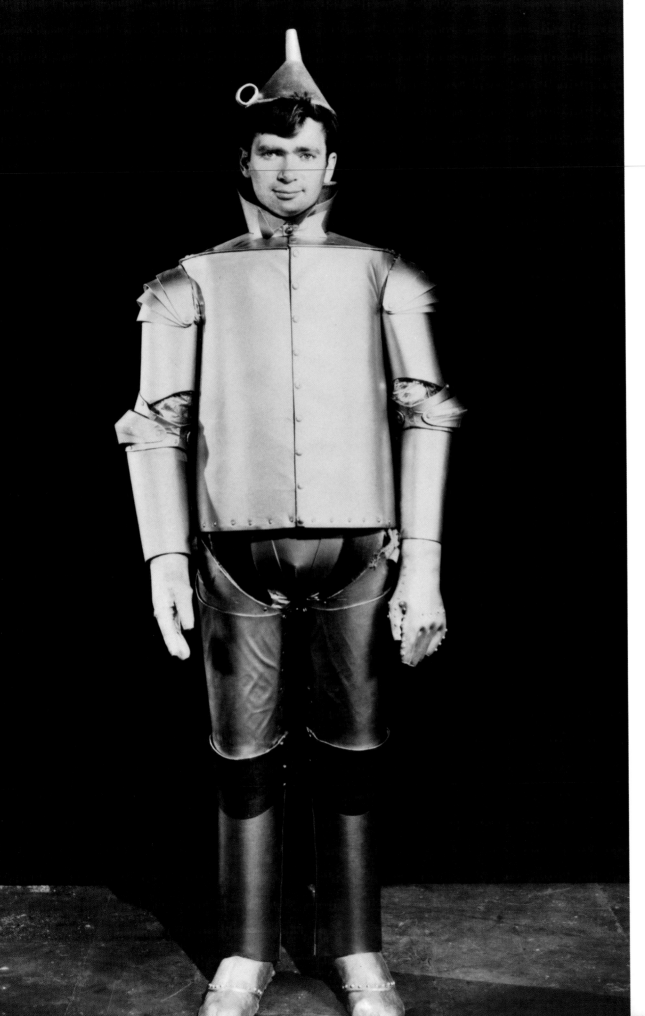

Buddy Ebsen, *a talented vaudeville-heritage hoofer like Ray Bolger and Jack Haley, had appeared in several movies in the 1930s, and was thought to be an excellent candidate for Scarecrow; eventually, though, he donned the Tin Man suit (left). He participated in early filming, but on October 21, 1938—nine days into the shoot—he suffered a brutal allergic reaction from breathing the aluminum dust that was in his makeup; he wound up in the hospital for two weeks, then had to recuperate at home for an additional month. Aluminum paste replaced the dust, and Haley replaced Ebsen, whose scenes were reshot. But here's some wonderful trivia: The man who would go on to TV fame as Jed Clampett and then Barnaby Jones does live on in the* Wizard *soundtrack. It is he harmonizing with Bolger and Judy Garland on "We're Off to See the Wizard" after Dorothy has oiled the Tin Man back to action. Opposite: Garland, in an early costume test for a dress wisely not chosen.*

GEORGE ZENO COLLECTION

"DOROTHY"
JUDY GARLAND #2

10/31/38
original Dress

BISON ARCHIVES (2)

Four more costume tests, *here and on the following two pages. Above: Garland, in yet another non-blue-gingham-check dress.*
Opposite: Bert Lahr (whose outfit was made out of real lion fur and was, under the lights, ferociously hot).

BERT LAHR
LION
3rd MAKEUP

10-8-3

BISON ARCHIVES

MGM/KOBAL/ART RESOURCE, NY

Above: *A flying-monkey actor displaying his wings. Opposite Gale Sondergaard. Hers is a most interesting story even amidst a field of* Wiz *tidbits as colorful as an acre of poppies. The native Minnesotan won an Academy Award for her very first film appearance in 1936's* Anthony Adverse. *In '37 she starred with Paul Muni in* The Life of Emile Zola, *and in '38, when MGM first thought it wanted a glamorous Wicked Witch of the West, she was cast. But when her own wardrobe test as an ugly witch turned the producers' heads, she balked at being so hideous, fearing it would damage her career. Sondergaard was out and, at the last minute, Margaret Hamilton was in. Later, in 1946, Sondergaard received a second Academy Award nomination for playing the king's principal wife in* Anna and the King of Siam. *Hamilton had to settle for screen immortality. On the pages immediately following: Garland works with Toto (actually, the female brindle Cairn terrier "Terry") so that they'll get along when the cameras are rolling. The canine actress makes $125 per week. Many Munchkins are paid $50 a week; some lucky few are taking home a hundred.*

MGM/PHOTOFEST

BISON ARCHIVES

BISON ARCHIVES (2)

The filming of what would become a deluxe $3 million movie had many goals, principal among them, on the heels of Walt Disney's 1937 instant classic Snow White and the Seven Dwarfs, *to prove that live actors could succeed at fantasy as readily as could animation. The true magicians of* The Wizard of Oz *were often behind the scenes, and perhaps no comment so confirmed their technical success as a line from* Time *magazine's August 21, 1939, review of the film. Opining that the filmmakers "left out only the kitchen stove," the critic wrote that* The Wizard of Oz's *"tornado rivals Sam Goldwyn's* The Hurricane." *Opposite: Shooting the title art in the Optical Department. Above: Blanche Sewell, the film's editor.*

BISON ARCHIVES

The Emerald City: *This, too, was ready for rendering. Baum first saw it as all green—green glass, lots of emeralds, shops selling all-green products, a green-lemonade vendor outside, children buying their drinks with green pennies—but he lightened up in later books with varying colors, and by 1938, Victor Fleming and his associates could present what they thought best. In Baum's novel* The Emerald City of Oz, *the city has nearly 10,000 buildings (actually, precisely 9,654) and nearly 60,000 citizens (actually, 57,318). In the movie, Oz is more compact and concise. Interestingly, it is probably related to the Chicago World's Columbian Exposition—the Chicago World's Fair— of 1893, which commemorated the 400th anniversary of Christopher Columbus's landing. Baum had moved to Chicago in anticipation of that extravaganza and was inspired by the fair's "White City." His illustrator W.W. Denslow followed on from pictures he had made for the* Chicago Times *of the White City. And, so, then: The Emerald City, the Windy City.*

In the forest of a Southern California soundstage, Haley, Garland, Bolger and Terry are about to meet Bert Lahr, the Cowardly Lion. Native New Yorker Lahr, like his fellow actors in Dorothy's trio of escorts, had a background in burlesque, vaudeville and on the legitimate stage, but was considered less of a dancer, more of a comic actor. His métier was stage musicals, and throughout the 1930s he was on the boards in a string of hits, culminating in turns opposite Beatrice Lillie in The Show Is On (1936) and Ethel Merman in the original production of Cole Porter's Du Barry Was a Lady—a bigger hit on Broadway in 1939 than The Wizard of Oz would prove in movie houses. Lahr was inspired in his depiction of the Cowardly Lion by performances in the Three Stooges flicks by fellow vaudeville veteran Curly Howard. Lahr was the only performer in The Wizard of Oz, Garland included, to be given two solos—"If I Only Had the Nerve" and "If I Were King of the Forest"—and of course is best remembered for that movie today. Very incidentally, the cartoon character Snagglepuss's identifying line—"Heavens to Murgatroyd!"—was first featured by Lahr in the 1944 movie Meet the People. *His true home was not on the big screen, however, but the stage, and in the 1950s he had a remarkable triumph when he was the surprise choice to star in the U.S. premiere of Samuel Beckett's* Waiting for Godot. *The run was short-lived, but the critical acclaim that greeted Lahr's performance endures.*

BISON ARCHIVES

*By **mid-autumn** in 1938, all of the ingredients had been assembled or decided upon and the cameras were rolling. The casting had finally been accomplished after many chapters, the sets had been constructed or were envisioned. Right: Munchkinland, on Stage 27.*

MGM/PHOTOFEST

FLEMING
PROD. 1060   SET NO. 10

Cross Road
Land
of Oz

MGM/PHOTOFEST (2)

Opposite: *The Scarecrow's field along the Yellow Brick Road, on Stage 26.* Above: *All those gnarly trees everywhere. As for the pathway: It has been, ever since Baum invented "the road of yellow bricks," a living cultural metaphor. It represents the quest and the promise and whatever else an individual chooses to ascribe to it. In the books, it had a companion throughway heading elsewhere, a road of red bricks. In contemporary times, it has been employed as a useful signatory by everyone from Elton John to Eminem, Captain Beefheart to the Arctic Monkeys, Oprah Winfrey (her success is "a yellow brick road of blessings") to Lady Gaga in "Gypsy" ("took a road to nowhere on my own / Like Dorothy on the yellow brick / Hope my ruby shoes get us there quick").*

BISON ARCHIVES

The Wizard's private room, *above. If there was an element that was more crucial than any other, it might have been the look of the ruby slippers. Smartly discarded was one of those tested on Garland's right foot (opposite). The curled-toe, so-called "Arabian Pair" was once owned by actress and memorabilia collector Debbie Reynolds, and sold for just over a half-million dollars when Reynolds's estate was auctioned in 2011. Deemed best-in-show by the moviemakers was the pair we see in action on the following pages, where more stories are told.*

MGM/PHOTOFEST

Iconic footwear . . . iconic footpath . . . iconic actress. The executives at MGM couldn't be sure of any of that during filming, and certainly weren't sure of it after the movie opened with something of a ripple but hardly a splash. We will delve further into the film itself in our next chapter, and into its reception in the chapter following. For now, more fun facts about these slippers. They were imagined as silver in L. Frank Baum's novel The Wonderful Wizard of Oz *(which had, by the late 1930s, undergone a title change, losing its "Wonderful"). But color—specifically Technicolor—was going to be a huge part of the MGM* Wizard of Oz, *arriving with a bang just as Dorothy's house did in Munchkinland. And so it was decided that ruby would pop better on the screen than silver. Once the color and Gilbert Adrian's design had been decided upon (Adrian was MGM's top costume designer), several pairs were fashioned by the Innes Shoe Company of Los Angeles. They were sized between 5 and 6, and between widths B and D (Garland found the larger pairs more comfortable). It's not certain how many shoes were made in all—six or seven pairs isn't a bad bet—but it is believed five pairs, four of them used during filming, survive today, with the best tracking device being the amounts they fetch at auction. Three of these pairs have felt cloth fastened to their soles, this to hush the sounds of Garland's dancing down the Yellow Brick Road. The most famous surviving pair is called "The People's Shoes," and can be seen at the Smithsonian National Museum of American History in Washington, D.C.; tradition holds that these slippers were featured most often in the film. The narrow 6B pair might have been made for Garland's double in the film, Bobbie Koshay. During a large auction of MGM props in 1970, much of this footwear was discovered in storage, and since then the story of the ruby slippers has taken a turn: It's all about money now. The Smithsonian's slippers were probably the ones that sold for $15,000 back in '70. In 1988 a pair sold for ten times that, and in 2000 an auction at Christie's saw the gavel brought down on a sale of $666,000—including the buyer's premium, of course. (In our chapter on Judy Garland, we will divulge the auction price of the blue gingham dress.) In 2012, Leonardo DiCaprio and others acquired a pair for the Academy of Motion Picture Arts and Sciences for an undisclosed sum. Lady Gaga, who used* Wizard of Oz *motifs in her massive Monster Ball Tour, said she had received a pair as a gift, but when it was found that the price tag had been perhaps 40 grand, the shoes' provenance was immediately suspect. Lastly: The irresistible allure of the ruby slippers is such that, in 2005, a pair graciously on loan to the Judy Garland Museum in Grand Rapids, Minnesota, was stolen—snatched, purloined, pilfered. What a wicked thing to do.*

MGM/KOBAL/ART RESOURCE, NY

The WIZARD of OZ

And now the film unfolds on the screen, one brilliant
scene after another. Sure, it's sentimental at times; sure, it's
melodramatic. But we remember every minute of it,
and always want to revisit those moments in Kansas,
Munchkinland and the Emerald City. Here we go!
*Opposite: When the movie was released, MGM was hoping
for an enormous international hit for the ages. That
wasn't to be the case at first but would be eventually. This
reissue, silver-anniversary poster features all the now-
famous selling points, from the stars to the songs.*

EVERETT

Today, the film seems perfect. But as opposed to books, which often represent the vision of one author, movies are team efforts. MGM's *The Wizard of Oz* was built in many stages, as Richard Corliss and our previous chapters have explained. Here's what you will not see in the following 32 pages, because Victor Fleming, having labored mightily, nevertheless turned in a 120-minute movie. *Gone with the Wind* was going to get away with its 238-minute run time in 1939, but a family film like *The Wizard of Oz* was not going to be allowed two hours. So said producers Arthur Freed and Mervyn LeRoy before three previews in California, which they hoped would help shave 20 minutes from the final product. Cut, in two stages, were:

• The now legendary musical number "The Jitterbug." It was a remnant retained from an already discarded subplot involving a Princess Betty and a Grand Duke of Oz. It was such a lively thing, it was clung to by Fleming and company. Finally, however, it just didn't make sense and had to go. Still, in the final movie, the Wicked Witch of the West tells her monkeys: "Send the insects on ahead to take the fight out of them!" The infectious "Jitterbug" number lives on today in a hundred licensed grade-school stage productions of *The Wizard of Oz*. The kids and their families love it.

• A significant portion of Ray Bolger's original dance sequence in "If I Only Had a Brain."

• Two reprises: one of Garland singing "Over the Rainbow" a second time and one of the Emerald City throng returning to "Ding-Dong! The Witch Is Dead." The "Rainbow" reprise was sung by Dorothy thinking about home in Kansas while imprisoned in the Witch's castle. Garland (and crew members) were so affected by the performance they teared up. Nevertheless: the cutting-room floor.

• A scene in which the Tin Man suffers the indignity of being

---

*Left: **At the Gale home*** *in Kansas, the tension between saintly good and abject evil is established as Auntie Em tells Dorothy that she must yield Toto to Miss Gulch, while Uncle Henry looks on. The actors are Clara Blandick, Garland, Margaret Hamilton and Charley Grapewin, the last of whom came out of retirement to join the cast. Auntie Em and Uncle Henry were the only Kansas characters to not be reincarnated in Oz, though for a time it was considered that Blandick would become the Good Witch of the North. Ultimately, the moviemakers wanted someone more glamorous, and Billie Burke was hired as Glinda.*

GEORGE HOMMEL/MGM/KOBAL/ART RESOURCE, NY

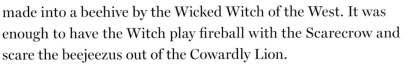

made into a beehive by the Wicked Witch of the West. It was enough to have the Witch play fireball with the Scarecrow and scare the beejeezus out of the Cowardly Lion.

• A Kansas scene in which the character Hickory (played by Jack Haley, and due to transmute into Oz's Tin Man) builds a tornado-fighting machine—which of course might have proved useful for Dorothy and the other Gales.

• A raft of insults and threats by the Wicked Witch of the West, who was plenty scary and detestable enough in shorter doses.

Finally the film sat at 101 minutes, and was released to the public. When it became so vastly popular through the years,

— ◆ ◆ —

While singing "Over the Rainbow," Judy Garland wasn't overly constrained by the uncomfortable corset she was forced to wear as Dorothy to hide her young womanliness. The actress, who would go on to be appraised by many as the greatest entertainer who ever lived, was 16 years old but already a veteran of half a dozen pictures when she filmed The Wizard; her age was one argument for those who wanted the younger Shirley Temple in the lead role. Her rendition of "Over the Rainbow" in that stunning (and stunningly mature) contralto voice is certainly a primary reason this was chosen in 2004 as No. 1 on the American Film Institute's 100 Years 100 Songs list. Now: We have already mentioned that a reprise of the song was cut from later in the film. But consider this: MGM almost dropped "Rainbow" altogether. Some of the filmmakers felt the Kansas sequence early in the movie was going on too long, or that the ballad was too slow and sophisticated for the kids, or that Garland should not be seen singing in a barnyard. Fortunately, wiser heads prevailed and the Harold Arlen–E.Y. Harburg composition, which won the Best Song Oscar in its day, has become the very definition of an American classic. A final note about the photographs we see on these pages: Obviously, they are sepia-toned, not pure black-and-white. So were the Kansas scenes in the original release of the movie. Interestingly, MGM rereleased the film in theaters in 1949 in black-and-white rather than sepia. Over the decades when The Wizard of Oz became an annual fixture in our living rooms—not least because of the nation's millions of black-and-white televisions in the 1950s and '60s—audiences figured the movie's Kansas was a black-and-white state. MGM never fought the assumption and issued hundreds of publicity photos and trailers in black-and-white. During a major restoration of the film in 1988, the sepia-tone footage was meticulously recovered. Still, though, Warner Bros., now owners of the film, released trailers for the large 1998 theatrical rerelease with Kansas rendered in black-and-white.

MGM/KOBAL/ART RESOURCE, NY

EVERETT

especially after hitting American television screens, all sorts of legends cropped up about what you were actually seeing. For instance, in a famous bit of lore: After Dorothy and the Scarecrow meet the Tin Man, and the trio continues on the road to Oz singing "We're Off to See the Wizard," some trees on the right of the screen waver. The conspiracy theorists have long posited that a crew member or perhaps one of the Singer Midgets was committing suicide by hanging. Actually, a large bird in the branches was exercising its wings.

So, then: five directors, many makeup problems, a couple of actor switches and a ton of angst later, *The Wizard of Oz* premiered in August of 1939 in Wisconsin, then in Los Angeles and then New York City. Highlights of what the audiences at Grauman's Chinese Theatre and the Capitol Theatre saw—and you have certainly seen—now unspool in our pages. Enjoy!

◆

The funny thing about Margaret Hamilton, seen here as Miss Gulch before she went all green and Wicked Witch on us, is that she was one of the sweetest and best-loved members of the cast. An example from behind the scenes, regarding Frank Morgan, who played the Wizard and who was also a personable actor: Whenever Hamilton witnessed the scene where the Wizard is awarding mementos of achievement to Dorothy's escorts—a medal of courage for the Cowardly Lion, a ticking heart for the Tin Man, a diploma certifying the intelligence of the Scarecrow—Hamilton would become emotional because, as she later said, "Frank Morgan was just like that in real life, very generous." (Hamilton had acted with Morgan earlier in 1937's Saratoga.*) A native of Cleveland, Hamilton had been a schoolteacher before becoming a character actor, and was thrilled when offered a role in Oz at the last minute: "I was in need of money at the time, I had done about six pictures for MGM at the time and my agent called. I said, 'Yes?' and he said 'Maggie, they want you to play a part on* The Wizard.' *I said to myself, 'Oh, boy,* The Wizard of Oz! *That has been my favorite book since I was four.' And I asked him what part, and he said, 'the Witch,' and I said, 'the Witch?!' and he said, 'What else?'" She actually played two witches—she's the Wicked Witch of the East in the tornado sequence—in addition to playing Almira Gulch of Kansas. It's good that she had three roles (only Morgan had more: five!), because at the end of the day, this nice woman was just too effectively malevolent, and several of the Wicked Witch of the West's scenes were trimmed or dropped because Hamilton's overall performance was deemed too frightening for the little ones in the audience.*

Kansas huckster *Professor Marvel, one of five fabulous characterizations by actor Frank Morgan in* The Wizard of Oz *(we'll detail the others on page 109), counsels—sort of—Dorothy, but soon enough the tornado will appear and the girl's future will be in the hands of fate. Morgan was billed right after Judy Garland in the famous movie, and in fact this is fitting, for in Baum's books, the character of the Wizard, and his earlier, very ordinary life in Nebraska (not Kansas) is as interesting, complicated and important as any. Oscar Zoroaster Phadrig Isaac Norman Henkle Emmanuel Ambroise Diggs (the Wizard's full name, its initials signifying OZ and then PINHEAD) uses some of his down-home magic tricks to prop himself up as the "great and powerful" once he accidentally lands via hot-air balloon in Oz. Much as Arthur Conan Doyle could not rid himself of Sherlock Holmes when he tried to kill him off at Reichenbach Falls, then was forced by his intense— insane!—readership to bring him back from the grave, Baum had the Wizard give up his throne at one point but was forced by public opinion to return him to subsequent books. In the later volumes of the Oz novels, Diggs introduces Oz to something like mobile phones and something like intelligent taxicabs. So maybe Professor Marvel was a wizard after all. In the 2013 hit Disney prequel, the man from the Midwest played by James Franco is indeed called Oscar Diggs, not Professor Marvel.*

RONALD GRANT ARCHIVE/TURNER ENTERTAINMENT/MARY EVANS

The Wizard of Oz *was not the first color film released by Hollywood, but its abrupt switch from sepia to three-strip Technicolor, which was truly state-of-the-art (actually, still at the experimental stage), was surely the most effective use of the rainbow medium yet. To create the effect of the house falling from the sky (opposite, top), a miniature house was dropped onto a painting of sky, then the film of that sequence was reversed so the house was rushing toward the camera. Bottom: The Wicked Witch of the East has been crushed, hard by the Yellow Brick Road.*

EVERETT

MGM/KOBAL/ART RESOURCE, NY (2)

EVERETT

Billie Burke *had a rare distinction at MGM in the 1930s: She had a principal role, as Glinda the Good Witch of the North, in one of its best-remembered films of the decade, and she was portrayed by Myrna Loy in a movie that won Best Picture for 1936. Born in 1884, she started as a stage actress and continued to prefer work on the boards even after acting in movies, because at least in the theater your voice would be heard (the films of the early decades of the century were, of course, all silent). She was noticed, in a big way, by Broadway impresario Florenz Ziegfeld Jr. and they wed in 1914. She spent most of the next few years on Broadway, but after the stock market crash of 1929 depleted the family fortune, Burke returned to the big screen in director George Cukor's 1932* A Bill of Divorcement *and his 1933* Dinner at Eight. *Ziegfeld died during the making of the former film, and in '36, MGM memorialized him in* The Great Ziegfeld, *with Loy as Burke and William Powell as her husband. In 1937, Burke was in* Topper, *starring Cary Grant and Constance Bennett, and the following year was called to Oz. She had it easier than Margaret Hamilton since, being a good Witch, she could float into Munchkinland in an elegant safe-as-safe-could-be bubble; Hamilton, disappearing in a torrent of fire, suffered second- and third-degree burns while filming and had to convalesce during the production. It's interesting that in Baum's novel Glinda is the Good Witch of the* South. *She is the Land of Oz's most powerful enchantress, yes, but there are others, including a Good Witch of the North. In the movie, all Good Witchiness is incorporated in the Billie Burke character. She helps Dorothy with the slippers, shows her the way to the Yellow Brick Road, wakes her with snowfall in the poppy field and of course, in a climactic scene in Oz, coaches her on how to head home.*

MGM/KOBAL/ART RESOURCE, NY

RONALD GRANT ARCHIVE/TURNER ENTERTAINMENT/MARY EVANS

WARNER BROS./AP

MGM/KOBAL/ART RESOURCE, NY

The Munchkins (opposite) are given their star turn at this point in the film, and if the moviemakers kept debating how much "Over the Rainbow" was too much, it is clear they decided early on: We can't have enough of the Munchkins. Dorothy, here, is clearly charmed by the revue that is being authorized for her entertainment by the town fathers (opposite, top), which includes the hoofers of the Lullaby League (bottom). Above: West is none too pleased by North's intervention (or her apparent power), particularly when, left, she uses her wand to bequeath Dorothy the slippers: "There they are, and there they'll stay."

RONALD GRANT ARCHIVE/WARNER BROS./MARY EVANS

MGM/KOBAL/ART RESOURCE, NY (3)

Dorothy is on her way *and the first soldier to join her crusade is Ray Bolger's Scarecrow. We said just a few pages ago that Billie Burke had the distinction of playing in* The Wizard *and having someone play the role of Billie Burke in MGM's* The Great Ziegfeld. *Well, Bolger played the Scarecrow and earlier had played* himself *in* The Great Ziegfeld. *In vaudeville and on Broadway he was sufficiently known as a fabulous dancer that the casting was de rigueur.*

RONALD GRANT/WARNER BROS./MGM/MARY EVANS/EVERETT

Jack Haley *had much better luck with the adjusted Tin Man makeup than poor Buddy Ebsen had, though he did suffer an eye infection that caused him, like Hamilton, to miss time during the shoot. As with Bolger, Haley was an Irish American from Boston who made his earliest fame with his feet; he also had a comic flair. He knew Garland, too, before he signed on to replace Ebsen: They had appeared together in* Pigskin Parade *in 1936. (Jack Haley Jr. would be married to Garland's daughter Liza Minnelli for five years in the 1970s.) In* The Wizard of Oz, *Haley used his regular speaking voice when portraying the Kansan Hickory, then went up an octave and added the lilting sweetness as the heart-seeking Tin Man. All of the costumes were difficult to perform in, and you'd get a debate as to whether the Tin Man's or Cowardly Lion's was more onerous (all of those flying monkeys are also-rans because they didn't appear in nearly as many scenes). Years later it was suggested to Haley that filming* The Wizard of Oz *must have been loads of fun. "Like hell it was," he answered. "It was work!"*

MGM/KOBAL/ART RESOURCE, NY

MGM/PHOTOFEST

Finally the fab four, *and once Dorothy wipes the tears from Lion's eyes they will continue their march—well, their communal skip—toward Oz. So many lines, some of them near-throwaways, and so many half-songs from this oft-viewed movie have entered the cultural lexicon: "my little pretty," "the great and powerful," "I'm melting" and so on. As we all remember, when the trio makes its way through the forest, where they will soon meet the Cowardly Lion, the melodic acceleration of Dorothy's "lions and tigers and bears—oh my!" is disproportionately memorable to the length of the scene. The phrase, which alludes to a fear of an unknown, lurking future, has been appropriated by everything from a comic book series about a boy and his stuffed animals to a hit R&B song.*

EVERETT

SILVER SCREEN COLLECTION/GETTY (2)

The poppies! *Baby boomers who grew up on* The Wizard of Oz *had great nudge-nudge sport in their college years with the fact that what felled Dorothy and company en route to Oz was the flower from which opium is derived. The subtlety these guffawing kids missed: Our heroes weren't users, the Wicked Witch of the West was a pusher, and she slipped them the mickey. Regardless, Garland sleeping in a field of red poppies and yellow flowers makes for a lovely picture. Opposite: They've made it to Oz, but their work is far from done. The Gatekeeper is played by the ubiquitous Frank Morgan, and for a fuller story of his contributions to this movie and Hollywood in general, please turn the page.*

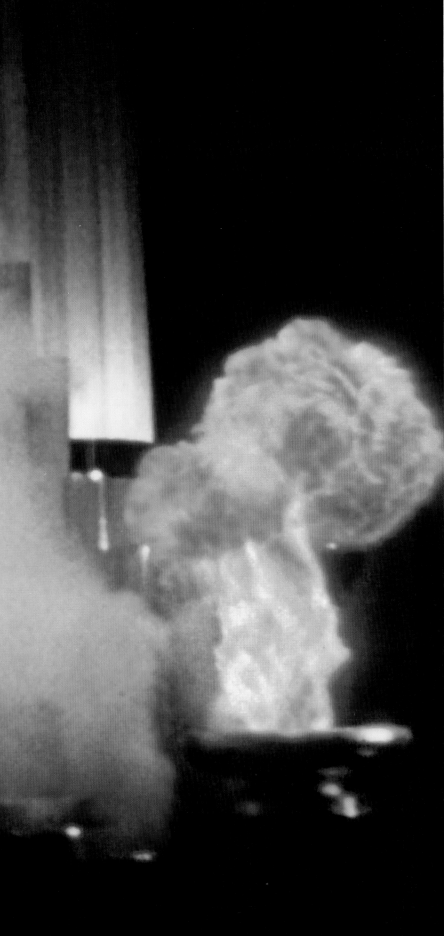

MGM/KOBAL/ART RESOURCE, NY

•◆•

Frank Morgan *was a cut above. He wasn't simply a "character actor" or a "contract player" or any of the other shorthand terms that defined many a career during Hollywood's Golden Age. The native New Yorker, youngest of 11 children, also—like so many of his* Wizard *confreres—began on Broadway, but bowed in movies when still in his mid-20s, debuting in* The Suspect *in 1916 and then, the next year,* Raffles, the Amateur Cracksman *alongside his buddy John Barrymore. He would be nominated for two Academy Awards, for Best Actor in 1935 for* The Affairs of Cellini *and in 1943 for Best Supporting Actor for his work in* Tortilla Flat. *MGM felt Morgan was so useful they signed him to a lifetime contract. And put him to work they did (he, too, was in* The Great Ziegfeld, *and also* Hallelujah, I'm a Bum; The Shop Around the Corner; The Human Comedy; The White Cliffs of Dover *and on and on). They never pushed him harder than during* The Wizard of Oz. *Yes, yes: They had envisioned W.C. Fields as the Wizard and he wanted $100,000 while they wanted to pay him $75,000. And, yes, they offered the role to Ed Wynn (remember him floating up to the rafters in laughter in* Mary Poppins?), *who turned it down. But they always had Morgan in their back pocket, and lucky them. He was Professor Marvel back in Kansas and then, once the story moved to Oz, the Gatekeeper of the Emerald City, the coachman of the carriage drawn by the Horse of a Different Color, the Guard at the entrance to the Wizard's hall and, finally, behind the curtain: the Wizard himself. He was also, of course, the floating, fiery head seen here that greets Dorothy and her quaking trio, and sends them off on their impossible mission, which is essentially to dispatch the Wicked Witch of the West. Morgan was wonderful and never purposely scene-stealing at every turn. While we are looking at this picture: a last word about the pyrotechnics on display in this movie. Morgan escaped unscathed, but Margaret Hamilton suffered severe burns to her face and hand when leaving Munchkinland in fiery fashion, and then her stunt double Betty Danko was severely burned—11 days in the hospital, legs permanently scarred—when a smoking pipe that was supposed to be a broomstick exploded. It was a different era. "I'm not suing you," said Hamilton, "because I know enough about this business to know I won't work again if I do sue. But I won't go near fire again." Well, there would continue to be fire aplenty, but Hamilton wouldn't be involved in the filming of those scenes.*

EVERETT

They tremble so, *and well they might, for separating the Wicked Witch of the West from her broom is as daunting a task as any ever assigned; consider that this Witch ranks fourth on the American Film Institute's all-time movie villain list, behind only Hannibal Lecter, who ate people's faces off; Norman Bates, of* Psycho *fame; and Darth Vader, who was . . . well, Darth Vader. So: A child, a Scarecrow who can't scare crows, a creaky Tin Man and a Cowardly Lion are going to confront such evil? They tremble as they enter the castle, but then, like Harry and Hermione and Ron will do in a filmic generation to come, they summon the nerve to confront their demon.*

The filmmakers *kept ratcheting back how terrifying the Witch's presence—or shadow—should be, and they couldn't be sure when they released the picture that they had got it right. Margaret Hamilton, for one, suggested that she wouldn't return for any sequel, not just because she didn't want to be typecast but because she was conscious of how much her performance might have disturbed children, whom she, as a former teacher, cared for deeply. (The point about a reunion movie was made moot anyway by the first film's cost overruns and Judy Garland's ascension to superstardom.) In years to come, Hamilton tried to make amends for the nightmares she had caused. She appeared on* Sesame Street *as a witch and later appeared on* Mister Rogers' Neighborhood, *where she showed the kids that the hat was just a hat, her performance was just a performance, and the whole thing was fantasy anyway.*

MGM/KOBAL/ART RESOURCE, NY

MGM/KOBAL/ART RESOURCE, NY

The grass is hardly greener for Dorothy in the other person's yard. She has found the Witch, but for whom is the hourglass sifting? This is the apotheosis of a movie climax: It's paced perfectly (which is to say, swiftly) and then, as we see in the three photos here, not only do we share in the emotional tug of people not present, represented by Auntie Em, but also the confusion of victors who don't yet understand quite what they've done—or how in heaven water can be more potent than fire. What a world, what a world, indeed. The audience is left breathless.

EVERETT

SILVER SCREEN COLLECTION/GETTY

RONALD GRANT/TURNER ENTERTAINMENT/MARY EVANS/EVERETT

MGM/KOBAL/ART RESOURCE, NY

MGM./KOBAL/ART RESOURCE, NY

Bad Wizard, good Wizard. *Certainly if anything is too pat about the ending of* The Wizard of Oz, *it is how easily the Frank Morgan character gets off the hook. But then, he's the only way out for Dorothy (seemingly), and Morgan has made his shiftiness evident and almost endearing since the original Kansas scenes. Professor Marvel, the Wizard: He's the Music Man before Robert Preston incarnated him, he's Elmer Gantry with a redemptive streak. Anyway, Toto causes a change in plans, as we know, and thank goodness Glinda arrives to introduce plan B (above).*

"There's no place like home" is the simple homily that, with a few clicks of the heels, sends Dorothy on her way—or, at least, out of her dream.

MGM./PHOTOFEST (2)

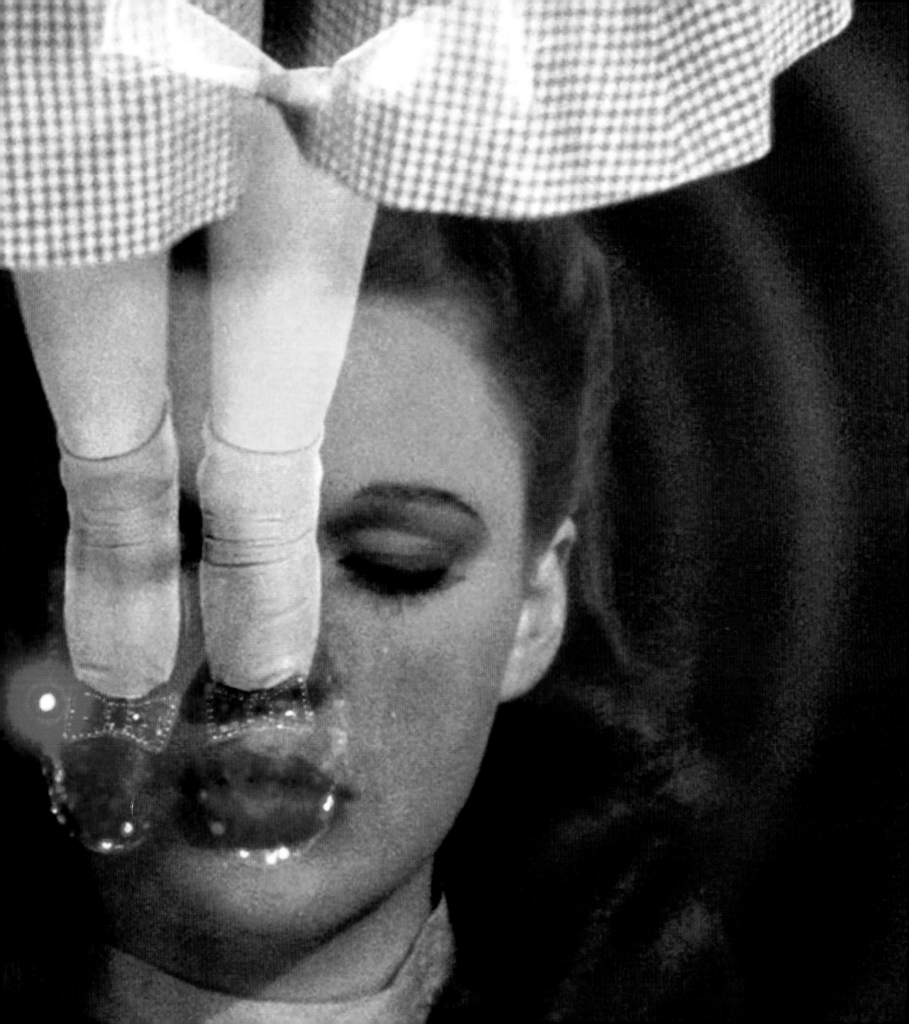

RONALD GRANT ARCHIVE/MARY EVANS

Where am I? *Or, more to the point: Where in the world was I? Glinda's way home worked, and Dorothy awakens to a host of loved ones (even Professor Marvel, at the window, now firmly part of the fold). The argument can be made, and so we will make it here, that not since Shakespeare has so much alter-ego role-playing been so successful in a dramatic or comedic endeavor. Often, there might be one or two folks incarnated elsewhere by mistake, or an attempt made at something larger that turns out to be a mess, but in* The Wizard of Oz *the games-playing is seamless, and the payoff priceless. When* The Wizard *was broadcast on television once a year in the 1950s and '60s, representing something of a national holiday, with parties planned and relatives invited over with their kids, there was no greater joy for the parents than watching their children as the scene depicted here played out: the little ones seated on the floor squealing with delight, "He was the Cowardly Lion!" "Hickory! Hickory was the Tin Man!" L. Frank Baum, years before, had written a perfect or near-perfect fantasy. MGM had made a perfect or near-perfect movie. All that had to happen now, in 1939, was to turn on the projectors and it would be the greatest and most deserving hit ever— bigger than Disney's* Snow White and the Seven Dwarfs! *Guaranteed. Right?*

Not Exactly
BOFFO

Well, no, the answer to the question posed on the
previous page is: Wrong. *The Wizard of Oz* was
not what you would call a blockbuster when it burst from
the gate. It wasn't even what you would call a hit.
But in its television afterlife, without changing the movie
a bit—no "director's cut"—it evolved into one of the
biggest and greatest films of all time.
Opposite: A photo from The Wizard's *glory years.
This is once the film has become an annual TV celebration,
and clearly this little girl, in her special* Wizard *dress,
is ready for the annual showing. Today, how many Dorothy
blue-check dresses are still sold in the Halloween
season is incalculable.*

AD LIB STUDIOS/MARY EVANS

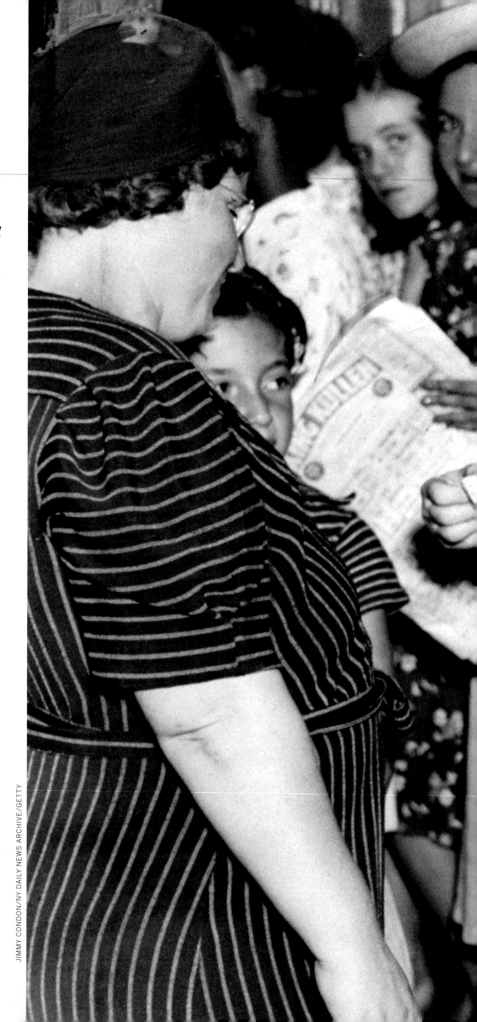

J ust as stunning to MGM's bean counters as a house falling out of the heavens and flattening a random witch was the reception *The Wizard of Oz* received in 1939. Disney's *Snow White and the Seven Dwarfs* had, just recently, become the biggest movie ever (and Disney had then angled to make an animated *Wizard of Oz*, only to be rebuffed because MGM held the rights to the book; Disney would get around to its animated *Return to Oz* in the 1980s and was also behind the recent James Franco feature—we'll get to all that). But the short of it: *The Wizard of Oz* opened to great fanfare, but then it sort of drifted on.

It did fine with the critics, okay with the audience. Frank S. Nugent, the esteemed screen-writer and subsequently *The New York Times'* respected and feared film critic, averred that the film was "a delightful piece of wonder-working which had the youngsters' eyes shining and brought a quietly amused gleam to the wiser ones of the oldsters. Not since Disney's *Snow White* has anything quite so fantastic succeeded half so well." He knew something; he had hit on something with the kid/parent thing—but that magical thing would not be firmly tapped into until much later, when families could focus on *The Wizard of Oz* in the seclusion of their own comfortable postwar homes.

After the success of Mary Martin's *Peter Pan* on TV in 1955, CBS decided to telecast *The Wizard of Oz* on November 3, 1956. As Richard Corliss has noted in his essay earlier in this book, *The Wizard of Oz* was instantly ascendant as some kind of American classic. There is a

— ◆ —

Some folks did go to see the film at the movie theaters, surely, and surely many were amazed. Here, there is a line waiting to get in to a showing at Broadway and 51st Street in New York City. The photograph says two things: The Wizard's hope to appeal to adults and not just to children seems to have been playing out. And also: When the Depression had flattened America in the prewar years, and many were unemployed, going to the movies with a precious nickel or dime was a requisite escape. The several great movies of 1939 fed that need.

JIMMY CONDON/NY DAILY NEWS ARCHIVE/GETTY

cliché about actors and actresses becoming overnight successes after years of hard work. This was the film equivalent: a movie being rediscovered (or, really, *discovered* by many who didn't even remember it) after 17 years. *The Wizard of Oz* would never go away again. It drew a larger audience on its second TV screening in 1959, and *The Wizard* was off and flying. In subsequent years, CBS yielded to NBC, then *The Wizard of Oz* went to the WB network. Some of the Turner cable channels showed it and . . . well, let it suffice that, as it celebrates its 75th birthday, it is the principal "old" family movie still broadcast regularly on TV. And the family still gathers.

Why?

Perhaps because we have had time to assess and reassess it (which makes you wonder how many truly great films have been lost to initial lack of interest or the erosions—the changing tastes and concerns—of time). Corliss explains a lot of this, and he has never been alone in the critical community in trying to parse not just why *The Wizard* was able to come back but why it has worked as the years have rolled on and society has changed so greatly. It's something of a singular, remarkable case, these critics agree. Like many fine works of art, they finally conclude: It touched the human core. "*The Wizard of Oz* has a wonderful surface of comedy and music, special effects and excitement," the late film critic Roger Ebert wrote when listing the film as one of his Great Movies, "but we still watch it six decades later because its underlying story penetrates straight to the deepest insecurities of childhood, stirs them and then reassures them."

Now, we still watch it seven and a half decades later—for all the same reasons.

DAVID GAHR

*Coming to **Oz** was an interesting American journey. In 1939 the Tin Man is a quickly conceived figure in the annual Macy's Thanksgiving Day Parade in New York City (opposite), and, propelled by the buzz that has attended the movie and its Munchkins, in that same burgh at eight a.m. on August 17, a crowd of 10,000 people, mostly women and children, surround an entire block to wait in line for an early screening (top; they do not all get in). But then the ardor cools for some reason; certainly intense competition from other fine movies, including family fare about Andy Hardy and Shirley Temple's* The Little Princess, *factored in. The next chapter: Starting in 1956,* The Wizard *begins a 57-and-counting-year run as an annual tradition on television (above, Margaret Hamilton coming right out of the screen and into youthdom's fragile psyche), and kids and parents everywhere agree: Hey, this is a wonderful movie!*

BETTMANN/CORBIS (2)

Judy

JUDY

Judy

Here we celebrate the great Garland,
who journeyed from Oz down a winding Hollywood
road that made her famous and beloved but that
regularly brought travail.
*Opposite: Iconic movie, iconic character,
iconic actress . . . and an iconic blue gingham dress,
which sold at auction in Beverly Hills,
California, in 2012 for $480,000.*

MGM/KOBAL/ART RESOURCE, NY

The tiny woman—not quite five feet tall—from Grand Rapids died of a barbiturate overdose in London in 1969. The writer Budd Schulberg bade farewell in the pages of LIFE: "Judy Garland was a little Mozart of song and dance. Of all the child stars who came out of the '30s, a classic period for talented moppets, only Judy Garland somehow survived of the first magnitude—a Lady Lazarus who kept rising from the dead, from countless suicide attempts and broken marriages and nervous breakdowns and neurotic battles with weight and sleep, to somehow pull her jangled nerves together, take command of the Palladium or the Palace or Carnegie Hall and bring down that audience one more time.

"When she was good, meaning when she was there, she was so very, very special that we laughed with her and cried with her and begged her for more in a marriage of requited love never before experienced in the theater. And when she was bad, which meant when she was ill, when she was atremble with indecision, when the steps wavered and the voice cracked in its diehard reach for the high notes in the rainbow, then her love, the audience turned on her in its righteous and wretched wrath and pelted her with rolls and bread and crumpled cigarette packs—as in that nightmare performance in her precious London not so long ago.

"And so she took her final curtain call last week, as used as she was loved, as exploited as she was revered, sentenced to martyrdom and sainthood in a show-biz world that cries too easily but shies from the true cause of the tears that Judy has been crying from Andy Hardy days onward."

Judy Garland was 47 years old. Her legend continued.

———— ◆ ————

Onstage at her smashing Carnegie Hall concert in May 1961, Garland is awash in waves of requited love.

JOHN LOENGARD

In the year of The Wizard, *1939, Mickey Rooney, Jack Haley (who of course played the Tin Man) and Garland share a microphone during a radio broadcast from New York City's Waldorf Astoria Hotel. (Fun footnote: Much later in life, Rooney would play the Wizard in a Broadway musical version starring Eartha Kitt.) In this period just before the United States entered World War II, MGM was working Rooney and Garland to the bone. After filming was finished on* The Wizard of Oz *on March 16, 1939, Garland reported back to work on May 12 to star opposite Rooney in the film version of the Broadway musical* Babes in Arms. *That movie wrapped on July 18, then the studio sent the two teenagers off on a cross-country promotional tour. On August 17, when* The Wizard *premiered at the Capitol Theater in New York City, they were sent to Gotham and asked (told) to do five shows a day from the stage in between screenings of the film. Then* Babes in Arms, *for which Rooney would be nominated for a Best Actor Oscar, premiered on October 13 and turned out to be a huge hit. And that, for these two kids, was just 1939!*

SNAP/REX USA

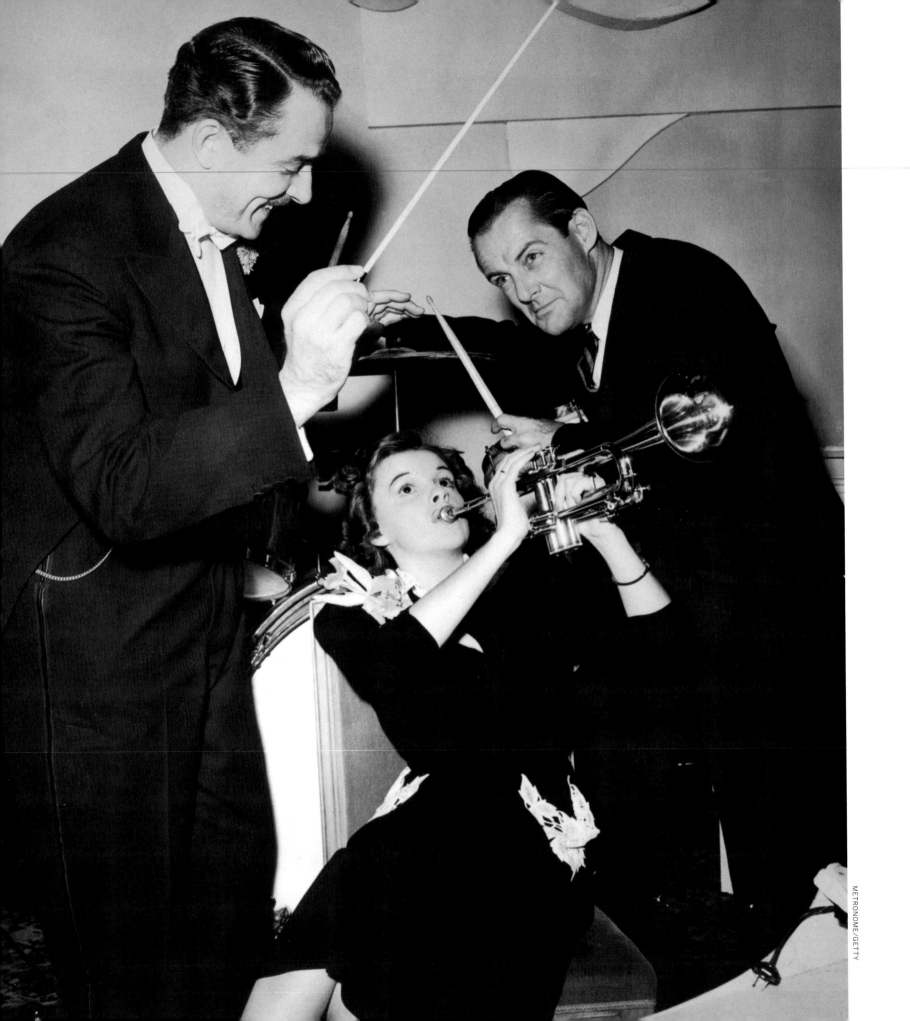

METRONOME/GETTY

HERBERT GEHR

In 1940, Judy blows her horn as bandleader Glen Gray (opposite, left) and Hollywood columnist Jimmie Fidler faux-accompany her in the Palm Court of San Francisco's Palace Hotel. Above: That same year, Judy sings "Over the Rainbow" to the CBS radio audience during the grand opening of the Arrowhead Springs Hotel in San Bernardino, California.

HERBERT GEHR

BETTMANN/CORBIS

Garland would marry *five times. In 1944, she is seen, above, with her date, the director Vincente Minnelli. They would wed the next year, and on the opposite page Judy is seen with their daughter, Liza. Garland and Minnelli would divorce in 1951.*

GEORGE SILK (2)

WARNER BROS./KOBAL/ART RESOURCE, NY

ALLAN GRANT

"**A Star Is Born,** *the year's most worrisome movie, has turned out to be one of its best," writes* LIFE *in our 1954 cover story (opposite). "In it onetime teenage star Judy Garland, now 32 and out of movies for four years . . . makes a film comeback almost without precedent." Above, top row: Two scenes from the movie with costar James Mason. Bottom left: Chilling on the set with Mason. Bottom right: Arriving for the September 1954 premiere with friends Lauren Bacall and Frank Sinatra.*

LIFE

REG. U. S. PAT OFF.

JUDY GARLAND TAKES OFF
AFTER AN OSCAR

FROM HIS FRIENDS:
THE REAL WILLIE MAYS

JUDY AS A GAMIN

20 CENTS

SEPTEMBER 13, 1954

In November 1958 *in Las Vegas, Judy joins her pals Dean Martin and Frank Sinatra for a Rat Packy moment. With Sinatra, you were in or out, and Judy was always in, as was Tony Bennett, who shared a revealing anecdote with* LIFE's *Robert Sullivan: "It's just moments before I'm about to walk out onstage for opening night at the Empire Room at the Waldorf, here in New York. All of a sudden I get a call. It's Judy Garland. She's on the phone, telling me that she's at the St. Regis Hotel and she's being beaten up—a domestic thing or something. And I don't know what to do. My ex-wife says to me, 'Call Frank.' He was at the Fontainebleau in Miami. I call him up. He had just finished making the movie* The Detective, *so he knew all the detectives and all the police who had helped with the movie. I tell him, 'Frank, Judy Garland's getting beat up at the St. Regis. I don't know what to do.' He says, 'I'll call you back in a few.' I go and do my show, and after it's over, Judy calls me up. 'I asked for help,' she says, 'but this is ridiculous. There's five lawyers in my suite and 900 policemen outside in the street.' And then Frank calls me up and says, 'Was that all right, kid?'"*

ALLAN GRANT

JOHN LOENGARD

CORNELL CAPA

Four final photos, *here and on the next two pages: Twirling onstage at the Palladium in New York City in 1951 (opposite) and triumphing in the same city a decade later at Carnegie Hall. Following pages: With Liza in 1964 and in a portrait made for* LIFE *by Milton Greene in 1961.*

GLOBE/ZUMA

PHOTOGRAPHED BY MILTON H. GREENE © 2014 JOSHUA GREENE. WWW.ARCHIVEIMAGES.COM

The CLASS *of* '39

That we remember *The Wizard of Oz* so well is extraordinary when one looks back at all the greatness it competed against in the greatest-ever movie year. The country was still in the dumps. Hollywood was not. *Opposite: In* Gone with the Wind, *Vivien Leigh and Clark Gable—not to mention the burning of Atlanta—brought the heat. Elsewhere in '39, Leigh's future husband, Laurence Olivier, was making hearts race in* Wuthering Heights.

EVERETT

MGM was almost working in the shadows with *The Wizard* (if anyone can ever work in the shadows in L.A.), because everyone in Hollywood—or anyone paying attention to Hollywood—realized that an even larger effort was being exerted in MGM's Civil War drama based on the best-selling Margaret Mitchell novel *Gone with the Wind*. That would prove a pretty fine and successful picture, to be sure, but much else would hit the screen in 1939, too—an astonishing bulk of it nothing short of wonderful.

Nineteen thirty-nine has been called the movies' best year ever, and few would choose to dispute the claim. These days, there are as many as 10 Best Picture nominees each year, but that is to juice TV ratings: keep the fans of more films interested until midnight. In '40 there were 10, too, but please ask yourself which of the other eight, besides *The Wizard of Oz* and *Gone with the Wind* (which would win), you might exclude: *Dark Victory, Love Affair, Mr. Smith Goes to Washington, Ninotchka, Of Mice and Men, Stagecoach, Wuthering Heights* or *Goodbye, Mr. Chips*. The similarity of the films ended with their uniform greatness; they were from all over the map: adaptations of fine fictions (historical or not), romances, fantasies, musicals, westerns. And the comedy, *Ninotchka,* starred Garbo! The great stars—Gable, Bogart, Davis, Cagney, Fonda, Grant, Stewart, Wayne and, yes, young Garland—were featured in more than one movie each that year, and the Best Director category featured Frank Capra, Victor Fleming (who would win not for *Wizard* but *Wind*), John Ford, Sam Wood and William Wyler. How busy were these talented folks? Well, we've already talked about the

❖

No, that's not John Wayne *on the horse in* Stagecoach. *It is his colleague Tim Holt, receiving instruction in Utah's Monument Valley—or just listening to tall tales—from his director John Ford, in a photograph that is marvelously illustrative of Hollywood's Golden Age. File under: You can't make this up.*

UNITED ARTISTS/PHOTOFEST

BISON ARCHIVES

RKO RADIO PICTURES/PHOTOFEST

five directors who pitched in at various times on *The Wizard of Oz,* and two of them—Fleming and George Cukor—worked on *Gone with the Wind* as well. Hollywood, in 1939, knew how to put movies together.

It wasn't just the Oscar-aspirant films, and it wasn't only studio pictures that were noteworthy, either. Shirley Temple in *The Little Princess* and Mickey Rooney in both *Andy Hardy Gets Spring Fever* and (alongside his pal Garland) *Babes in Arms* had enormous successes. Also, the year saw: *Confessions of a Nazi Spy, Intermezzo: A Love Story, Jesse James* (a box office smash), *Midnight, On Your Toes, Only Angels Have Wings, The Roaring Twenties, They Made Me a Criminal, Young Mr. Lincoln, Gunga Din.* Much further afield, the French cineast Jean Renoir's *The Rules of the Game* was released in 1939 as well.

What is our point? Perhaps that too much has been made in previous assessments about the fact that *The Wizard of Oz* wasn't, in its year, an earlier *Star Wars* or *Lord of the Rings* or *Harry Potter*—not commercially. It was attempting to shuffle into a very crowded field. That so many of these films are remembered today when in '39 every showing of *Gone with the Wind* was chewing up four hours of a viewer's time (intermission figured in) is astonishing. Many, many people in filmmaking were at the very top of their games.

We are not small-minded, and we love movies. And so, even in this volume celebrating *The Wizard of Oz,* we pause to celebrate 1939 itself: a year in movies unlike any other, before or since. The studio system was well in place, technologies were improving, smart folk were at work; World War II hadn't yet culled their ranks. Competition was healthy—actors and directors and even producers were pushed to be adventurous because so many others were vying for the precious few coins American moviegoers had to offer.

The result of that wonderfully complicated equation was glorious.

❖

Hard at work *we see, on this page from top, James Stewart between takes of* Mr. Smith Goes to Washington *and director George Stevens on the set of* Gunga Din. *Opposite: Three of the year's heroes, Cary Grant, Frank Capra and Stewart during the filming of* Mr. Smith Goes to Washington. *Grant of course starred as well in* Gunga Din.

COLUMBIA/KOBAL/ART RESOURCE, NY

Here we see Humphrey Bogart on the set of Dark Victory *with Bette Davis and Geraldine Fitzgerald. In 1934, there was an unsuccessful stage play about a woman—a fast-lane socialite with a taste for fast cars, fast men and fast horses—who would go blind and die, meanwhile finding love with the doctor who was treating her. It closed after a little more than a month. No matter, screenwriter Casey Robinson adapted it, Davis was cast in the lead; Fitzgerald was her character's best friend; George Brent signed on as the doctor; and Bogie played a stablehand. After inking her pact, Davis's real-world marriage to Ham Nelson failed, as did her relationships with lovers William Wyler and Howard Hughes, and she begged off, claiming illness. "Stay sick!" said the studio, having seen the terrific early rushes. The film was a hit, and even the often curmudgeonly Frank S. Nugent of* The New York Times *wrote, "A completely cynical appraisal would dismiss it all as emotional flim-flam, a heartless play upon tender hearts by a playwright and company well versed in the dramatic uses of going blind and improvising on* Camille. *But it is impossible to be that cynical about it. The mood is too poignant, the performances too honest, the craftsmanship too expert. Miss Davis, naturally, has dominated—and quite properly—her film, but Miss Fitzgerald has added a sentient and touching portrayal of the friend, and George Brent, as the surgeon, is—dare we say?—surprisingly self-contained and mature. This once we must run the risk of being called a softy: We won't dismiss* Dark Victory *with a self-defensive sneer." The film lost Best Picture to* Gone With the Wind; *Davis lost Best Actress to Vivien Leigh; the movie's musical score lost out to that of* The Wizard of Oz. *But in 1939, everything made of celluloid seemed fairy-dusted.*

WARNER BROS.

Elbowing for attention *in 1939 were, clockwise from top left, Rooney and Garland in* Babes in Arms; *Garbo and Melvyn Douglas in* Ninotchka; *and Laurence Olivier and Merle Oberon in* Wuthering Heights. *On the opposite page, top, is Robert Donat and schoolboys in* Goodbye, Mr. Chips, *then Rooney again and Lewis Stone making* Andy Hardy Gets Spring Fever.

MGM/PHOTOFEST

JOHN SPRINGER COLLECTION/CORBIS

20TH CENTURY FOX/EVERETT

Above: *Lon Chaney Jr. (left) and Burgess Meredith in* Of Mice and Men. *Opposite: Shirley Temple in* The Little Princess, *a bigger family-fare hit than* The Wizard of Oz *and one of the year's hugest hits.*

RKO RADIO PICTURES/PHOTOFEST

This still from *the movie* Gunga Din, *loosely based on the same-titled poem and other short stories by Rudyard Kipling, indicates something that is often lost in misconception: The movie was as much a comedy as an adventure. In fact, Cary Grant (far left) lobbied for his role because it would allow him to stretch and be funny. He got the part, and Douglas Fairbanks Jr. (left) had to settle for a less flamboyant assignment. The man in the middle here is Victor McLaglen. These three were British sergeants in the film who, along with their Indian water-carrier, Gunga Din, played by the not-the-least-bit-Indian Sam Jaffe, fight the native Thuggee— murderous gangsters roaming throughout colonial India. Everyone from Ben Hecht to William Faulkner pitched in on the script, but* Gunga Din, *which was directed by the estimable George Stevens, probably isn't as good as it is remembered to be. Even still, years later, Steven Spielberg gave it several literal or allusive shout-outs in the second of his* Indiana Jones *movies, which shared the comic/adventuresome spirit of* Gunga Din. *Apparently, what Spielberg was saying: Lots and lots of young boys had enjoyed it.*

Long Live the —◆
WIZARD!

The Wicked Witch of the West, like her evil sister of the
East, proved something less than immortal—to her
great dismay. Not so *The Wizard of Oz* itself, as a creation
of the mind and an enchantment of the masses.
*Opposite: At Madame Tussauds in New York City in 2010,
the Wizard of Oz 4-D Experience, which promises an
interactive Land of Oz, is drawing them in—probably better
than the MGM film did in Times Square in 1939.*

MARTIN ROE/RETNA/CORBIS

L. Frank Baum's *Oz*, which name he took from a filing cabinet he happened to glance upon that was labeled *O* to *Z*, has proved eternal. It has been diminished by some contemporary productions, elevated by others. But it remains, like all the greatest of great works, open to interpretation. Proof of this is that, even in the wake of the monumental 1939 movie, *Oz* formulations, permutations and procreations have continued—forcefully and regularly. Modern interpreters have not felt in any way cowed: They have not shrunk like the Wicked Witch after being doused in a bucket of water in the face of the Great Work. Why? Because Baum's *Oz* is a rich story with rich characters, and a moral that is at least a little ambiguous, and therefore ripe for fashioning and refashioning.

Today, *The Wizard of Oz* lives on in memory and also in plush dolls, a million cheaply made pairs of ruby slippers and probably as many replica Witch hats. That is as it should be. Any cultural touchstone that grows as huge will be imitated, replicated and bifurcated. This is a tribute; it is adjunct to the adage that the sincerest form of flattery is imitation. Are they imitating the view of Baum or MGM? That hardly matters. The larger point: You really have to go to something as big as the Beatles or Elvis to find an equivalent, as far as being a touchstone.

The Wizard, even more so than Elvis, John, Paul, George or Ringo, is wide open to both appreciation and appropriation. You can do what you want with *The Wizard of Oz*, and many have—and will.

Day in and day out, people with commercial interests sidle up to *The Wizard*. And then there are others, intellectually inspired by Baum or by the movie, who want

───────── ◆ ─────────

You never know where or when references to The Wizard of Oz *are going to pop up or set down. Outside the famous Harrods department store in London, the sad, dead feet of the Wicked Witch of the East are part of a promotion. The Witch's legs are the size of a double-decker bus, which is an easily understood measurement in England.*

REX USA

to carry more to the table. They bring imagination and even genius to bear (Gregory Maguire, the author of the novel *Wicked,* is one). They spin things forward like Dorothy did in approaching the Yellow Brick Road with eyes wide open. They entertain us all like Baum did.

The profiteers and the protean: There is nothing to be done about this. The Baum book has been in the public domain for some time and, as especially with such efforts as Maguire's *Wicked,* some of this is to be enthusiastically encouraged. Baum imagined a world that didn't exist but was alluring, and now other imaginative people fill it in different ways. That's a lovely thing.

Yes, sure: sometimes not. In spite of the talent involved, the Diana Ross–Michael Jackson film version of the stage musical *The Wiz* is to be given a miss. There are other productions and products it would be better to skip. But when your youngest child dons a Dorothy dress and heads out trick-or-treating, your heart thanks heaven for *The Wizard of Oz.*

L. Frank Baum imagined many, many wonderful things, but he never could have imagined this. Nor could he have imagined that more than a century after he found his best voice in this book, and 75 years after a great movie was made of it, anyone might be claiming that in the pantheon of American creativity *The Wizard of Oz* deserves a high, exalted place. Truly. *The Scarlet Letter, The Adventures of Huckleberry Finn, Moby-Dick, Ethan Frome, The Great Gatsby, For Whom the Bell Tolls, The Grapes of Wrath, The Catcher in the Rye* . . . Foster, Berlin, Ives, Gershwin, Presley, Springsteen . . . Stuart, Bierstadt, Rothko, Pollock, Warhol . . .

Why not Baum? Why not *The Wizard of Oz?*
Why not, indeed.
Long live *The Wizard*!

———————— ◆ ————————

English choreographer *Adam Cooper is an elegantly dancing Tin Man in a 2008 production of* The Wizard of Oz *at the Royal Festival Hall in London in 2008.*

SUZY DEL COMPO/CAMERA PRESS/REDUX

JOAN MARCUS/AP

Ballets and plays and movies, oh my! *Opposite, clockwise from top left: Kristin Chenoweth (left) and Idina Menzel in the original Broadway production of the musical* Wicked, *based on Gregory Maguire's novel; the kickoff of the world tour of* The Wizard of Oz on Ice *in St. Louis in 1995; and the Broadway production of* The Wiz *in 1975. This page, clockwise from top left: Journey Back to Oz (1974), with a Witch voiced by Ethel Merman, a Dorothy voiced by Judy Garland's daughter Liza Minnelli and a Scarecrow voiced by Garland's great pal Mickey Rooney;* Tom and Jerry & The Wizard of Oz; *honorary mayor of Hollywood Johnny Grant, center in the black hat, celebrates the Munchkins as they receive stars on the Walk of Fame.*

ABC/PHOTOFEST

WALT DISNEY PICTURES/KOBAL/ART RESOURCE, NY

BUENA VISTA/KOBAL/ART RESOURCE, NY

New films *have introduced new characters.* The Muppets' Wizard of Oz *in 2002 found a role for Kermit the Frog (top) and the* 2013 *hit* Oz the Great and Powerful *starred James Franco as Oscar Diggs, who is seen here with China Girl, a doll from the village of China Town, where everything is made of, yes, china. Opposite: Fairuza Balk as Dorothy, six months after her return from Oz, in 1985's* Return to Oz. *She's having trouble sleeping. Perfectly understandable.*

Just ONE *More*

MGM/KOBAL/ART RESOURCE, NY

Good advice for us all: *Follow the Yellow Brick Road . . .*

3 1333 04239 4872

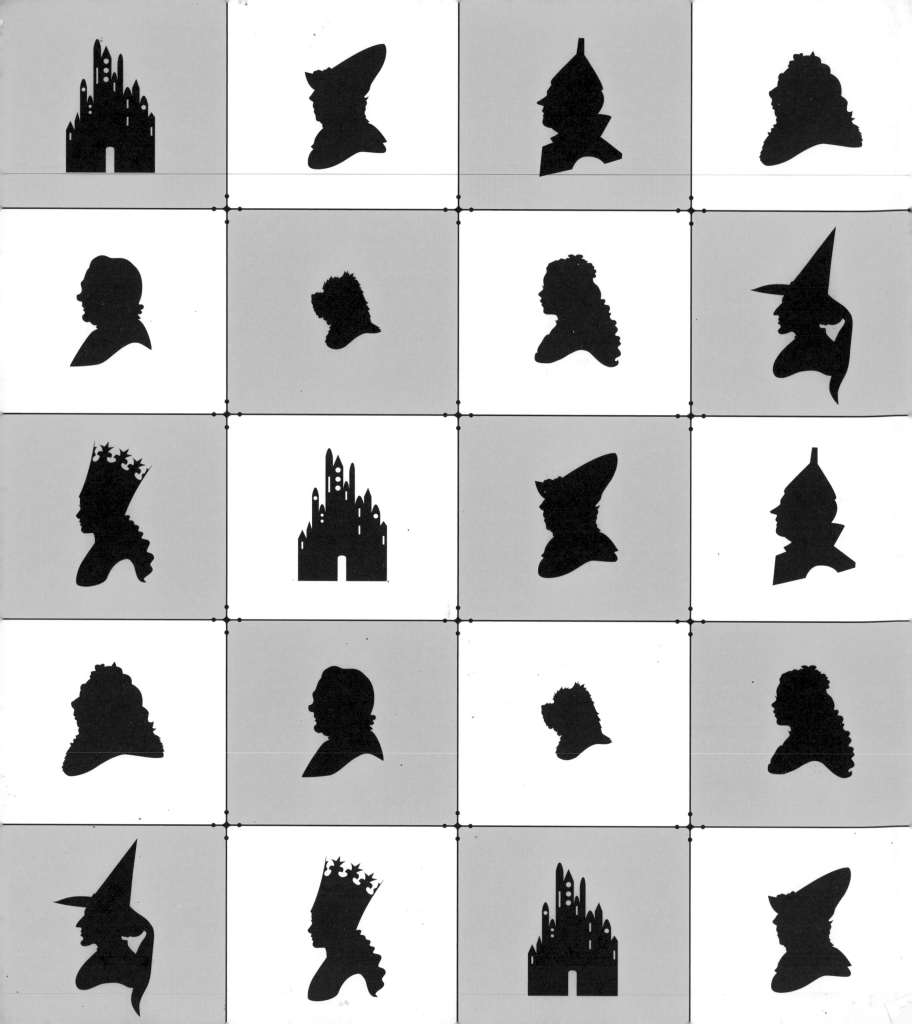